44 0

D1760366

University of
Hertfordshire
Library

Reference only

Tortious Liability of Statutory Bodies:
A Comparative and Economic Analysis of Five English Cases

Tortious Liability of Statutory Bodies: A Comparative and Economic Analysis of Five English Cases

Basil S. Markesinis
Jean-Bernard Auby
Dagmar Coester-Waltjen
Simon F Deakin
Foreword
by
Sir Sydney Kentridge KCMG, QC

•H A R T•
PUBLISHING

OXFORD – PORTLAND OREGON
1999

Hart Publishing
Oxford and Portland, Oregon

Published in North America (US and Canada) by
Hart Publishing
c/o International Specialized Book Services
5804 NE Hassalo Street
Portland, Oregon
97213-3644
USA

Distributed in the Netherlands, Belgium and Luxembourg by
Intersentia, Churchillaan 108
B2900 Schoten
Antwerpen
Belgium

Distributed in Australia and New Zealand by
Federation Press
John St
Leichhardt
NSW 2000

Hart Publishing Ltd is a specialist legal publisher based in
Oxford, England.
To order further copies of this book or to request a list of other
publications please write to:

Hart Publishing, Salters Boatyard, Folly Bridge, Abingdon Rd,
Oxford, OX1 4LB
Telephone: +44 (0)1865 245533 Fax: +44 (0)1865 794882
e-mail: mail@hartpub.co.uk

British Library Cataloguing in Publication Data
Data Available
ISBN 1 84113-124-5 (cloth)

Typeset by Hope Services, Clifton Hampden, Abingdon
Printed in Great Britain
by Biddles Ltd, Guildford and Kings Lynn

The Basic Principle of Tort Law:

Stated

"If [the child/claimant] can make good her complaints (a vital condition, which I forbear constantly to repeat), it would require very potent considerations of public policy, which do not in my view exist here, to override the rule of public policy which has first claim on the loyalty of the law: that wrongs should be remedied."

M v. *Newham London Borough Council* and *X* v. *Bedfordshire County Council* [1994] 2 WLR 55 at 532, per Sir Thomas Bingham MR

Confirmed but diluted in practice

"Sir Thomas Bingham M.R. took the view, with which I agree, that the public policy consideration which has first claim on the loyalty of the law is that wrongs should be remedied and that very potent counter considerations are required to override that policy . . . in my judgement there are such considerations in this case."

X (Minors) v. *Bedfordshire County Council* [1995] 3 WLR 152 at 183, per Lord Browne-Wilkinson

Challenged

"The trend of authorities has been to discourage the assumptions that anyone who suffers loss is prima facie entitled to compensation from a person . . . whose act or omission can be said to have caused it. *The default position is that he is not.*" (emphasis added)

Stovin v. *Wise* [1996] 3 WLR 388 at 411, per Lord Hoffmann

Foreword

This fascinating and original book is an exercise in comparative law. This is not a discipline which has traditionally appealed to English lawyers. In Trollope's legal novel *Orley Farm* the young radical lawyer explains that it would be pointless to obtain a translation of an eminent German lawyer's lecture

> ". . . seeing that we cannot bring ourselves to believe it possible that a foreigner should in any respect be wiser than ourselves. If any such point out to us our follies, we at once claim those follies as the special evidences of our wisdom. We are so self-satisfied with our own customs, that we hold up our hands with surprise at the fatuity of men who presume to point out to us their defects".

I do not suppose that there are many English lawyers who now have such an extreme distaste for foreign law. Nonetheless, we remain somewhat wary of other European legal systems. And we suspect that comparative law has little place in the practice of law in this country. This book should rapidly correct that view. It is an extremely practical book. It shows that comparative law can be "hard law". Any common lawyer will read it with interest and pleasure.

The authors analyse five modern English tort cases in each of which the courts have held that public bodies, such as the police and local authorities, are immune from liability in damages for allegedly negligent failure to exercise their statutory powers or perform their statutory duties. The judgements in these cases turn largely on considerations of public policy and are often based on a pessimistic forecast of the unhappy economic and administrative consequences which would flow from any other rule. Thus it has been said repeatedly that to allow actions against the police for failure to prevent crime, (however negligent the omission may seem to be) would be against public policy because, so it is said, it would not promote observance of a higher standard of care by the police but would result in the significant diversion of police resources from the prevention of crime to defence of legal suits. Similarly, one of the reasons given for refusing to permit actions against local authorities which fail to use their powers to make roads safer is that the authorities would adopt a defensive policy and spend less on education and social services.

Amongst the cases discussed by the authors are *Hill* v. *The Chief Constable of West Yorkshire*, *X (Minors)* v. *Bedfordshire County Council* and *Stovin* v. *Wise*. These well known cases have been much discussed in English legal journals. The originality of this book is that it examines comparable cases in which French and German courts have dealt with factual situations similar to those which faced the English judges. The authors ask, and try to answer, two questions. First, why have French and German courts on the whole rejected the policy arguments which have found favour with English courts? Second, does the imposition of liability on public authorities in situations where English courts would have found them immune lead to the unfortunate results predicted by the English courts?

In contrast to those lawyers who feel that little is to be learned from foreign legal systems there are those who think that what is done abroad must be superior – that we should for example import the French inquisitorial system and the American law of defamation. Needless to say, that is very far from being the approach of the distinguished authors. They analyse the French and German decisions as closely as they do the English ones. They are well aware, too, that it can be dangerous to invoke precedents from jurisdictions as different from our own as France and Germany without some understanding of the social and legal matrix within which the cases have been decided. They do not, however, hesitate to set out their conclusions. They prefer the judgment of Sir Thomas Bingham M.R. in *X (Minors)* v. *Bedfordshire County Council* to the judgments which ultimately prevailed, just as they prefer the dissenting judgment of Lord Nicholls of Birkenhead in

Stovin v. *Wise* to the majority judgments. The reader will form his or her own view of the cases discussed. But I do not believe that anyone who has read this book will in future accept, in the absence of real evidence, the confident predictions of the consequences which will follow the adoption of one or other rule of tort law.

An example of the type of confident prediction questioned by the authors is the one which has been used to justify the absolute immunity of the advocate for anything said, done or not done in court. In *Rondel* v. *Worsley*, in justifying this rule of absolute immunity, four of the five Law Lords cited *Munster* v. *Lamb (1883)* and in particular the statement of Brett M.R.:

> "If amidst the difficulties of his position he [counsel] were to be called upon during the heat of his argument to consider whether what he says is true or false, whether what he says is relevant or irrelevant, he would have his mind so embarrassed that he could not do the duty which he is called upon to perform."

In the nature of this decision it could hardly have been based upon any positive evidence. If the rule in *Rondel* v. *Worsley* is ever to be reviewed it might be useful to make a comparative study of the position in South Africa, a country where the legal profession is divided as it is in England and where advocates have the same duty to the court, to the client and to the public (including the cab-rank rule) as do counsel in England. In South Africa, as in other civil law countries, the advocate has no immunity from actions for negligence and in respect of defamatory statements made in court has only qualified privilege. The manner in which South African advocates have done their duty without the benefit of absolute immunity would show how hopelessly wide of the mark were the gloomy speculations of Brett M.R.

Went the Human Rights Act comes into force next year the various rules of immunity created by the judicial decisions discussed in this book will undoubtedly be re-evaluated, particularly in light of the decision of the European Court of Human

Rights in *Osman*. When that re-evaluation begins it will have no more useful starting point than this book.

Sydney Kentridge
London
23 September 1999

Preface

The question whether statutory bodies should be liable in tort towards persons harmed by their negligent actions or omissions is one that is currently occupying the attention of our courts. Paradoxically, the frequency of litigated incidents has grown even though our courts have, until very recently, been moving steadily towards a non-liability position through the use of "strike out actions". The practical significance of the subject is thus great and, if anything, going to increase, since the *Osman* decision of the plenum of the Strasbourg Court is likely to put English judges under increased pressure to modify if not to change their current stance.

To this practical aspect of our topic one must add a significant academic dimension: the subject straddles public and private law – a distinction which has always caused some difficulties to English lawyers – and presents a unique opportunity for an interdisciplinary analysis that can fruitfully combine ideas from other systems as well as economic arguments. The latter in particular must now be considered "fair play" for academics since some judges have, themselves, used them to justify their conclusions.

In this study, conducted under the auspices of the Oxford Institute of European and Comparative Law, four of us have combined our efforts with a view to bringing together our different interests and talents in the hope that this may help further the debate. We do so aware of the fact that no single book will help end the current debate given both the complexity of the issues involved and the fact that beneath these legal views lie deep philosophical opinions about the role of the state, the relationship between the courts and public administration, and the desirability (or dangers) of increasing civil litigation. These theoretically differing views are exemplified by the opinions of

Lords Bingham and Hoffmann - quoted at the very beginning of this book. Academics must, surely, be encouraged to join the fray when they see these judicial giants showing such signs of divergence!

The text of this book is accompanied by the translations of seven leading German decisions. Five texts come from the pen of Mr Raymond Youngs of the Southampton Institute of Higher Education, and two from that of Mr Tony Weir of Trinity College, Cambridge. Neither of these colleagues is, of course, burdened by our views, although they deserve our thanks as well as full credit for their acknowledged expertise in, among other things, the demanding art of legal translator. The same grateful thanks are extended to Mr Martin Matthews who gave us the benefit of his learning in both tort and administrative law matters as well as his well-known attention to detail, and to Mr David Howarth for a most valuable discussion of the relationship between tort law and liability insurance. Last and by no means least we record our gratitude to Sir Sydney Kentridge KCMG, QC, for contributing a Foreword to this book. How he finds time to practice and also oblige his friends who make such unreasonable demands on his time just before the summer holidays is a source of puzzlement. Yet those who have over the years had occasion to admire his work, know his keen interest in the academic aspects of the law, especially when human rights issues are involved. We thus suspect that this interest, coupled with his known generosity of spirit, encouraged him to lend to our book the invaluable imprimatur that comes with his great expertise in this area of the law.

Last but not least we express our sincere thanks to Hart Publishing and its staff for providing yet again the kind of prompt, professional, and efficient service that has been the hallmark of the founder.

Oxford, 15 August 1999

B S Markesinis
Jean-Bernard Auby
Dagmar Coester-Waltjen
Simon F Deakin

Contents

Table of Cases

The Authors

Jean-Bernard Auby is Ordinarius Professor at the University of Paris II (Panthéon-Assas), Faculté du Droit et des Sciences Economiques. He is Senior Teaching Fellow and Deputy Director (for French Law) of the Oxford Institute of European and Comparative Law (1998-2001) and a Visiting Fellow of University College, Oxford.

Dagmar Coester-Waltjen is Ordinarius Professor of Comparative Law at the Ludwig-Maximilians University of Munich and Director of that university's Institute of International and Foreign Law. She was Senior Teaching Fellow of the Oxford Institute of European and Comparative Law in 1998/99 and Visiting Fellow at Lady Margaret Hall.

Simon Deakin PhD is a Reader in Economic Law and Assistant Director of the ESRC Centre for Business Research at the University of Cambridge. He is a Fellow of Peterhouse, Cambridge.

Basil S Markesinis QC, DCL, D.Iur.h.c. (Ghent, Paris I, and Munich), is Clifford Chance Professor of Comparative Law at the University of Oxford and Jamail Regents Chair of Law at the University of Texas. He is a Fellow of the British Academy and a Corresponding Fellow of the Royal Belgian and Netherlands Academies and of the Academy of Athens. He is Founder Director of the Oxford Institute of European and Comparative Law and a Fellow of Brasenose College, Oxford.

1

A First Look at the Five Cases and the Problems they Raise

1. Introductory comments

One does not have to be either an advanced or sophisticated lawyer to appreciate the importance of our subject; but it might not be out of place to remind the reader of its complexities and how we tried to confront them. These stem from factors which one could describe as both philosophical and methodological. The philosophical factors ultimately turn round the model of justice one thinks most suited for the law of torts – corrective or distributive – and the way these starting points inevitably colour one's feelings that the contemporary law of torts is either becoming too mean or too generous. One can debate this to eternity; but, like most philosophical issues, it is, we feel, incapable of a definitive answer.

The methodological problems are easier to explain, although, again, not subject to one, obvious solution. Here are some reasons for this statement.

First is the fact that our subject straddles tort law and administrative law and, thus, when one is proposing solutions, one must bear in mind constantly the different philosophies, type of remedies and procedures that obtain in these two branches of the law. Secondly, and more controversially, this is one (of the many) areas of tort law that could benefit from both conceptual and empirical studies concerning the economic and insurance consequences of imposition of liability. That such studies are rare cannot be doubted (although the gap is slowly being filled, especially in the common law world). More regrettable, however, is the fact that for many traditional lawyers and, more so, for judges, the

1

desirability of adopting such an approach has not yet been proved beyond all reasonable doubt. Our view on this particular point is that some British judges have attempted such analyses, but in a manner that strikes us as being essentially intuitive. Continental courts are, if anything, even further behind ours in this respect (although this observation is subject to what we say below about German academic literature). We welcome the growing use of economics in the English courts and recognise that, since this development is still in its infancy, there is bound to be some degree of experimentation in the way the courts use this type of material. However, we will argue below that the courts should be aiming for a more principled approach to economic reasoning and to the assessment of economic evidence. Finally, one must note the added complexity introduced by our wish to discuss our subject in a comparative manner. Such a dimension is, we feel, essential if we are to assert, as we do in this book, two things: first, that English law is not only in an unsatisfactory state but is also set on a course of conflict with the law that is coming out of Strasbourg; and secondly, that the ideas and experience of French and German law which, arguably, lie at the heart of the Strasbourg approach, suggest that the liberalisation of the tort rules that Strasbourg might provoke will not entail catastrophic consequences in any economic or practical sense.

The need to add a comparative aspect to our study does not blind us to the dangers that come with any compressed presentation of foreign law and the ease with which this can (unintentionally) lead to distortions. On the contrary, because we are conscious of these dangers, we have tried to overcome these methodological difficulties by concentrating on five specific factual configurations which are not only important in daily litigation practice but have also revealed exact parallels in our three models: the English, the French and the German. This focused approach inevitably underplays (but does not ignore) other important features (e.g. level of damages, procedural devices) that affect the broader picture. To that extent our study can only, and with caution, support any wider theory about tort liability of public bodies in general. But legal theories, like buildings, are not constructed in one fell swoop but are the result of the careful positioning of one stone after the other in a fairly planned way. Thus, to change metaphors, we are confident that if the seeds of our research take root, and more colleagues – practising or academic – look at how different legal systems have coped with similar factual situations, more elaborate and differentiated products can eventually grow out of such efforts. This, then, is as much an essay on comparative methodology as it is a critique of the solutions adopted by English law.

It is also with methodology that we wish to close this section of preliminary observations. In this book, what will be particularly criticised is not so much the actual result reached by our courts in the five instances we have selected for discussion – although we readily confess our dislike of it – but the growing tendency to exclude liability through the utilisation of the notion of "duty of care". This concept, which has no real parallel in any of the modern civil law systems, is exceptionally vague and blunt. Its vagueness can either be used to conceal all meaningful discussion of the policy arguments that underlie these disputes or, conversely, turn the judicial process into an open-ended and unsubstantiated debate over value judgments. Either way, it seems to be encouraging our courts to impose, in practice if not in theory, blanket immunities, effectively preventing future litigants from asserting that the facts of their dispute justify a different legal outcome. For a long time English law has tolerated this essentially "unjust" result in the interests of what one could broadly describe as "administrative convenience". The growing constitutionalisation of private law, especially through the medium of human rights legislation, and the need for growing accountability, may, however, be about to defeat this peculiarity of English law. Not everyone will weep for the possible demise of a notion of duty of care which, fifty years ago, one great jurist[1] called the "fifth wheel of the coach" and which, nowadays, at least one contemporary specialist[2] has openly condemned as a superfluous cause of

[1] Buckland, "The Duty to Take Care" (1935) 51 *LQR* 637.
[2] Hepple, "Negligence: The Search for Coherence" (1997) 50 *Current Legal Problems* 69 *ff.*

confusion. But if that occurs – a big "if" at present – it will have been facilitated by influences which emanate from outside the area of private law and, more interestingly, outside the state boundaries of the English legal system. This line of thought will bring us back to our starting point about the overlap of public and private law – this time in the form of mutual interaction. But it will also place us within the realm of comparative law as we discover yet another pressure point for the growing convergence of the common and civil law systems. The last section of this book may thus, contrary to what was said earlier, justify some observations that extend beyond the specific facts of our five factual configurations.

2. Tort law and economic analysis: some general considerations

This work is not only comparative in nature. We thus also make use of the techniques of economic analysis to throw light on the legal issues under discussion. Since such an approach to law is not widely recognised in our three models, it might be useful, at the outset, to clarify some issues relating to the use of economics in legal scholarship. This is the aim of this section.

Economic analysis can be used in a number of ways to help us understand and evaluate decisions of the courts in relation to the tort of negligence. "Positive" economic analysis aims to identify the economic purpose and function of rules of legal liability, and to predict possible effects of changes in those rules. This is done, initially, by making certain behavioural assumptions about the responses of individual actors to rules of law. Individuals are assumed to act "rationally" in response to legal rules in much the same way as participants in market transactions respond to changes in prices. Legal rules, like prices, send signals about the likely consequences of behaviour, to which the parties are assumed to be capable of adjusting. By affecting the costs and benefits which attach to conduct of particular kinds, liability rules can influence both the "supply" of and "demand" for certain activities.

The precise nature of the initial assumptions upon which this type of reasoning depends is a matter of some dispute among law and economics scholars, many of whom would reject the notion that individuals always act with perfect rationality in the way that many textbook models of market behaviour imply. This is not the place to enter into this methodological debate;[3] it is sufficient for our purposes to note the claim made by the economic analysis of tort law – namely, that legal rules have behavioural consequences which can be modelled and predicted with varying degrees of confidence depending on the context in question.

"Normative" economic analysis seeks to evaluate legal rules against criteria of economic efficiency. The meaning of "efficiency" needs to be carefully considered in this regard. Essentially, an outcome is said to be economically "efficient" if the *overall wealth or well being* of society is enhanced. The branch of economics known as "welfare economics" has developed a range of sophisticated techniques for determining when this is or is not the case. A first step is to regard the welfare of society as synonymous with the aggregate welfare of its individual members. Situations can then be ranked according to how far a move from one to another involves an increase or decrease in the welfare of the individuals involved. A "Pareto-efficient"[4] move is one in which at least one person is made better off and no-one is made worse off; a "Pareto-optimal" allocation is a state of affairs in which no further improvements of this kind

[3] These methodological issues are considered by S Deakin, "Law *versus* Economics? Reflections on the Normative Foundations of Economic Activity" in M Richardson and G Hadfield (eds), *The Second Wave of Law and Economics* (1999). For a valuable recent overview of the law and economics movement by two of its leading exponents, see L Kaplow and S Shavell, "Economic Analysis of Law", National Bureau of Economic Research Working Paper No. 6960 (1999).

[4] The expression "Pareto-optimal" refers to the origin of this criterion of efficiency in the work of the Italian economist Vilfredo Pareto. For an important discussion of the use of the Pareto criterion in modern law and economics, see G Calabresi, "The Pointlessness of Pareto: Carrying Coase Further" (1991) 100 *Yale Law Journal* 1211.

can be made. A move is "potentially Pareto-efficient"[5] if the resulting allocation of resources increases the aggregate or over-all welfare of the group, even if, as a consequence, some individuals are left worse off.

In all this, the notion of "value" used by economists refers to the subjective preferences of individuals as revealed by their conduct and behaviour in situations of bargaining and exchange. Stated slightly differently, value is a function of the expressed "wants" of individuals. The reasons for the use of this definition are tied up with the historical development of economic methodology and with the rejection of attempts to derive indicators of value by reference to certain supposedly fundamental "needs".[6] Again, we must pass over some important methodological debates, which have called this predominant approach into question.[7] It is enough for present purposes to seek to clarify exactly what is being claimed when law and economics scholars refer to efficiency in the context of tort law. What they normally mean by "efficiency" is that a legal rule induces a reallocation of resources from less highly valued to more highly valued uses, thereby increasing the total welfare or well-being of all the individuals concerned. If this is done without diminishing the well-being of any particular individual, the outcome is Pareto-efficient; if some individuals lose out, but aggregate well-being is increased, there is potential Pareto efficiency.[8]

---

[5] Potential Pareto efficiency is also known as "Kaldor-Hicks efficiency" in the economic literature. See, e.g., R Posner, *Economic Analysis of Law*, 4th ed. (Little Brown 1993), ch. 1.

[6] This is discussed in S Deakin, "Law and Economics" in P Thomas (ed.), *Legal Frontiers* (Dartmouth 1997).

[7] See S Pratten, "Needs and Wants: the Case of Broadcasting Policy" (1998) 20 *Media, Culture and Society* 381.

[8] The emphasis in the study of the liability rules of tort law is on allocative efficiency as described in the text, but there are other notions of efficiency which do not depend on there being a redistribution or reallocation of resources which may be important in other contexts (such as company and commercial law): see S Deakin and A Hughes, "Economic Efficiency and the Proceduralisation of Company Law" (1999) 3 *Company, Financial and Insolvency Law Review* (Mansfield Press, forthcoming).

How is this general approach applied to tort law? The economic theory of law sees tort law as a means of reducing the overall costs of "accidents" and other causes of harm in society. As Calabresi puts it in his seminal work, *The Costs of Accidents*:

"apart from the requirements of justice, [it is] axiomatic that the principal function of accident law is to reduce the sum of the costs of accidents and the costs of avoiding accidents."[9]

According to Calabresi, accident costs are of three main types: (1) the costs to victims in terms of injury, lost earnings and other damage; (2) the costs incurred by both potential plaintiffs and potential defendants in taking precautions to avoid harm; and (3) the costs of administering the system of accident compensation, in terms of the processing of claims, the adjudication of disputes and the distribution of payments. Calabresi's point is that from the perspective of economic efficiency, the aim of the law should be to minimise the sum total of these costs. Minimising the costs of harm to victims may not be possible without curtailing other activities which society values. Similarly, the goal of full compensation for all victims of harm would imply an increase in certain administrative and organisational costs.

In short, the economic analysis of tort law tells us that hard choices are unavoidable when considering the degree of care to be demanded of the perpetrators of harms or the level of compensation payable to victims. The standards set by the law of tort are not just an indication of those types of action or activity which society finds reprehensible; they also tell us what level and distribution of harms society is prepared to tolerate in return for achieving some other end or goal. Against this background, the "positive" economics of tort seek to tell us how potential plaintiffs and defendants are likely to respond to rules of a particular kind, what the resulting degree and incidence of harm will be, and what knock-on effects are likely to flow from the attempts of the parties to adjust to particular liabilities (or to the absence of liability). This is a task which, while it can make a

[9] At 26.

certain amount of progress using axiomatic reasoning based on the model of the "rational" economic actor, can ultimately only be carried forward through empirical analysis. Fortunately for tort lawyers, the volume and quality of empirical research on the practical effects of liability rules have both increased in recent years, so that we do now have firm evidence on many matters which were previously the subject of speculation and hunch.[10]

The task of "normative" economics, in evaluating tort law against the criteria of efficiency, is in many ways much more problematic. To be completely sure that a particular outcome was allocatively efficient, we would have to engage in calculations of the costs and benefits of using the law to shift resources within and between particular groups. Because of the inherent complexity and difficulty of this type of calculation, law and economics scholars tend to fall back on a number of conceptual devices, which substitute for a more specific analysis. Here, the way in which liability rules are seen as countering "externalities" is a central issue. An "externality" is simply an external cost or benefit which is conferred or imposed on an individual as the result of the conduct of another. Put slightly differently, externalities are unbargained-for effects; they result from the inability of the parties concerned to bargain over the possible consequences for each other of their future conduct. An externality gives rise to a "social cost", which in this context refers to a category of cost that reduces the overall well-being of society. Externalities are thereby a cause of inefficiency in the allocation of resources.

This is the issue dealt with in R.H. Coase's classic article, "The Problem of Social Cost".[11] Coase argued that rules of private law, including what we now think of as "property rules" and "liability rules",[12] could operate in such a way as to offset

[10] See, generally, D Dewees, D Duff and M Trebilcock, *Taking the Facts Seriously. Exploring the Domain of Accident Law* (OUP, 1996).

[11] (1960) 3 *Journal of Law and Economics* 1; reprinted in Coase, *The Firm, the Market and the Law* (Harvard, 1988).

[12] The distinction between property rules and liability rules was introduced and systematised by G Calabresi and D Melamed, "Property Rules, Liability Rules and Inalienability: One View of the Cathedral" (1972) 85 *Harvard Law Review* 1089.

externalities, by imposing liabilities upon those responsible for inflicting unbargained-for harms upon others. However, it is essential to bear in mind here the distinction between "social cost" and "private cost". Coase was not arguing that it was always and everywhere efficient to compensate the victims of tortious harm. Not all private costs or harms give rise to a social cost. A true externality arises only when the parties are prevented from reaching a consensual solution by obstacles to bargaining, or "transaction costs".

The importance of transaction costs in tort law can be seen through an example. When a court imposes liability on a polluter, the issue for the economist (according to Coase) is whether the value of production in society as a whole is increased or decreased as a result of the court's intervention. This is because the imposition of liability on the polluter will cause a loss to him, which may outweigh the gain to those who were harmed by his activities. Seen purely from the viewpoint of efficiency (and leaving aside other, non-economic considerations which might be expected to influence the court), the issue turns on which of the two parties places the highest value on the right in question. If it were possible to bargain at low or zero cost, the court might assume that the victims of the pollution did not value their freedom from pollution very highly – otherwise they would have "bought out" the polluter. On this basis, it would opt for a finding of "no liability".

On the other hand, the court might take the view that the barriers to a transaction of this kind were in practice very considerable, with the result that there was no realistic prospect that bargaining would take place. (This would be a reasonable assumption in many cases of pollution where the threat of "free riding" deters coalitions of pollution victims from banding together to negotiate a solution with the polluter.) Under these circumstances, the solution most consonant with efficiency would be for the court to assign the right to the party who would have purchased it but for the existence of high transaction costs. If this would have been the pollutee, the court will impose liability on the polluter.

The search for efficiency in tort law is thus bound up in practice with attempts to conceptualise the related concepts of "externalities" and "transaction costs". Since much of tort law is concerned with liability between strangers, among whom bargaining is either expensive or impossible, the notion of externality is often highly relevant. However, externalities can also arise in many situations where the parties are known to each other in advance but where one can find incomplete information or similar barriers to efficient contracting. Here, liability rules may play an important role in promoting efficiency, and it may be largely a matter of legal history and accident that such rules are often grouped together under the heading of the tort of negligence rather than taking a contractual form. The "rigidity" of the English law of contract in respect of the protection of third party rights is thus one explanation for the existence of duties of care in tort which relate to pure economic loss.[13] In other areas where the tort–contract boundary is more fluid, as in the case of the rules governing the employment relationship, tortious duties overlap very closely with implied contract terms.[14]

Applying these ideas to the context of the liability in tort of public bodies, we are faced with a range of possible uses for the economic analysis of law. From a "positive" perspective, economic analysis can be used to tell us what the effects of decisions on liability might be in the three areas identified by Calabresi: the costs of harmful actions and activities; the costs of precautions taken to avoid harm; and the costs of administering claims for compensation. In other words, we may get a clearer idea of whether the imposition of liability is likely to lead to greater care being taken by public bodies, and whether this is at the expense of excessive precautions and/or high administration costs. From a "normative" perspective, economic analysis may be able to provide some indication of whether or not reallocations of resources, which result from liability rules, enhance efficiency. Is society bet-

---

[13] See B S Markesinis, "An Expanding Tort Law – the Price of a Rigid Contract Law" (1989) 105 *LQR* 104.

[14] See B S Markesinis and S F Deakin, *Tort Law* (4th ed., OUP, 1999), ch. 6.3.

ter off if public bodies are held responsible for the consequences of their action or inaction over a wide range of matters affecting the individual citizen, or would well-being be enhanced if individuals themselves were left to take the necessary precautions (through insurance or otherwise) to safeguard their interests?

In all this, it is just as important to be aware of what economic analysis cannot do. A first caveat of this kind relates to the role of positive or predictive economics. As we saw above, axiomatic reasoning of the kind used by economists to generate predictions or hypotheses is, strictly speaking, only the preliminary stage in a process of inquiry which should lead on to empirical studies of various kinds. In the absence of empirical research, which examines the operation of the law in concrete institutional and market settings, the predictions of purely conceptual economic reasoning would have to be treated with the utmost caution by the policy maker or judge.

A second caveat concerns the role of non-economic values in the process of policy formation and analysis. As we explained, welfare economics have developed a set of techniques, which help us in determining whether particular allocations of resources either enhance or diminish the overall wealth or well-being of society. Concepts such as "externalities" and "social cost" are aimed at providing a basis for understanding and resolving conflicts between private interests and the wider collective good. It is true that this kind of analysis would be of little value in certain societies and political contexts. This would be so, at one extreme, if society placed no value whatsoever on individual freedom and autonomy, or if, at the other extreme, it were completely indifferent to the consequences for third parties and for the wider community of private, self-interested behaviour. To that extent, therefore, the use of the techniques of welfare economics presupposes some agreement on a basic core of values in society; but we have no difficulty in suggesting that these are values which would be widely accepted in modern, liberal democratic societies.

In short, the criteria of economic efficiency cannot fail to be of interest and concern to judges and policy makers in societies such as our own. But this does not imply that economic efficiency is the only or sole set of values which should guide the law. What economic analysis cannot do is weigh efficiency in the balance against other, potentially competing values – such as equality in distribution, or respect for the dignity of the individual. In proposing the use of economic analysis, therefore, in the context of tort law, we must also insist that there is a proper appreciation of the limits – both methodological and normative – to this kind of reasoning. Without such an appreciation, economics can become a dangerous tool.

Consider, for example, the criterion of Pareto optimality, which we outlined above. In insisting that a move from one state of affairs to another cannot be deemed efficient unless it avoids making anyone worse off than they were before, the Pareto criterion appears to give maximum respect to individual autonomy: no one should be deprived of rights or resources against their will. But the Pareto criterion, in itself, is perfectly compatible with sets of allocations, which cannot be reconciled with liberal values. As the Nobel laureate Professor Amartya Sen has pointed out:

> "[a]n economy can be optimal in this sense, even when some people are rolling in luxury and others are near starvation, as long as the starvers cannot be made better off without cutting into the pleasure of the rich."[15]

Whether a Pareto-optimal state of affairs is truly desirable is, in the final analysis, a question that can be answered only by reference to values, which, as we have already indicated, lie beyond the scope of economic analysis.

An understanding of what economics can and cannot do in this context is all the more important because of the growing use of economic ideas by the judges themselves. Writers in the law and economics tradition have not sought to claim that the "inherent economic logic" of the common law is the result of explicit economic reasoning. Rather, they have suggested that "economic principles are encoded in the ethical vocabulary that

[15] A Sen, *Collective Choice and Social Welfare* (1970), 22.

is a staple of judicial language".[16] This is an important and interesting claim, although it is beyond the scope of our present discussion to consider it in any depth. Of more immediate concern to us are some signs that judicial antipathy to economic reasoning is weakening, and that some judges are increasingly prepared to make explicit reference to economic concepts when determining the scope of liability rules of private law. In the case of the tort of negligence, the foremost example of this is the judgment of Lord Hoffmann in *Stovin* v. *Wise*.[17] We return to a closer examination of Lord Hoffmann's use of economics, and to other references to economic reasoning in the five cases under review, in our discussion in the following chapters.

3. Tort liability of public bodies: the position in principle

(a) English law[18]

In this section we attempt a thumbnail sketch of the basic principles applicable to our three models, whereas in the next section we describe the five English factual configurations which have provided the parameters of this study. We must start by reminding ourselves that in this book we are concerned with a topic that straddles public and private law and that, in principle, a breach of a public law right will not give rise to a claim for damages unless the latter can also be based on a private law cause of action. It is further well settled that a breach of a statute, be it culpable or not, will not, of itself, give rise to a private law cause of action unless it is shown that the legislator, explicitly or by necessary implication, intended to create a private cause of action in favour of a class to which the plaintiff belongs. This

---

[16] W Landes and R Posner, *The Economic Structure of Tort Law* (1987), 23.

[17] [1996] AC 923, 941–58.

[18] For fuller discussions, see Arrowsmith, *Civil Liability and Public Authorities* (1992); Harlow, *Compensation and Government Torts* (1982); Street, *Governmental Liability* (1953) – full of ideas but out of date; Wade and Forsyth, *Administrative law* (6th ed., OUP, 1994); Weir, "Governmental Liability" (1988) *Public Law* 40 *ff*.

matter ultimately becomes one of statutory construction; and it would seem that, outside the area of workplace legislation, such private law causes of actions are very rarely discovered or invented. But could the carrying-out of a statutory duty by the defendant create a relationship between himself and the plaintiff such as to give rise to a duty of care at common law?[19] It is clear that, both in theory and in practice, the co-existence of a common law duty of care alongside a statutory duty is possible. It is equally clear that liability in damages cannot arise when the public body is doing what Parliament has "authorised". This means that if the decisions complained of fell within the ambit of the statutory discretion they cannot be actionable at common law. If, however, the decision complained of is so unreasonable that it falls outside the ambit of the discretion conferred by the statute, then there is no *a priori* reason for excluding all common law liability. However, as Lord Woolf MR recently said,[20] the prospect of establishing this *Wednesbury*[21] type of reasonableness is "extremely remote". Yet only if this hurdle is surmounted will the court then proceed to examine whether a common law duty of care can be established by applying the tripartite test of *Caparo*:[22] forseeability, proximity and fair, just and reasonable. In this context, one must not forget that this test was introduced to act as a three-element controlling device. This is precisely what it has become, especially since the courts allowed themselves the right to determine what is fair, just and

[19] We do not discuss here the possibility of a duty of care being imposed upon the authority's servants in the course of performing the authority's statutory functions. The point was, however, considered by Lord Browne-Wilkinson in *X (Minors)* v. *Bedfordshire County Council* [1995] 3 WLR 152, 185 *ff.*

[20] *Barrett* v. *Enfield London Borough Council* [1997] 3 WLR 628, 634. Unlike the *Bedfordshire* case, which concerned the extent of the duty of care owed by a local authority to children *prior* to their being taken into care, *Barrett* concerned the extent of the duty owed *after* a child had been placed in the care of a local authority. In this case, as well, the conclusion was the same: no liability for the reasons given in *Bedfordshire*. This result was reversed, however, by a unanimous House of Lords (see [1999] 3 WLR 79), and the case was remitted for trial.

[21] *Associated Provincial Picture Houses* v. *Wednesbury Corporation* [1948] 1 KB 223.

[22] *Caparo Industries Plc.* v. *Dickman* [1990] 2 AC 605.

reasonable by taking into account "the statutory framework within which the acts complained were done"[23], i.e., bringing the public law tests into the private law phase of the enquiry. Thus, despite numerous qualifying sentences found in the opinions of our judges, the combination of public and private law criteria has drastically limited contemporary ability to seek damages from negligent statutory authorities.

(b) French law

It is impossible to proceed and compare specific cases before stressing how different French and English law are in their approach towards the question of administrative liability. A bird's eye view of the main differences between these two visions can be given in the following way.

First, in French law, it has been accepted since the end of nineteenth century that administrative liability was not, as a rule, subject to the same rules as those applying to private liability. Thus, in one of the most famous French cases[24] the Tribunal des Conflits held that liability in the public services:

> "cannot be governed by the principles which are laid down in the Civil Code for relations between one individual and another; that this liability is neither general nor absolute; that it has its own special rules which vary according to the needs of the service and the necessity to reconcile the rights of the state with private rights."

Notwithstanding this statement, one must immediately stress that a considerable historical evolution has taken place since that decision was handed down defining the principles according to which administrative liability is submitted to special rules – belonging to public law – which are different from ordinary rules on civil liability. When the principle was stated in *Blanco* it meant, in the opinion of the Conseil d'Etat, that the administration would less easily and less frequently be held liable than

---

[23] See, for instance, *Stovin* v. *Wise* [1996] 3 WLR 388, 414–5, per Lord Hoffmann.

[24] Tribunal des Conflits, 8 février 1873, Blanco, *Recueil des arrêts du Conseil d'Etat*, 61, concl. David.

individuals according to the rules of private law. Nowadays, however, the special nature of administrative liability law has acquired a totally different meaning. On the whole, therefore, one can argue that this part of the law has become more generous to plaintiffs and more ready to accept the existence of liability than is private liability law. This inversion has become most visible in recent times and the question is, "what provoked it"? At this stage of our analysis, suffice it to mention only selected elements.

Sociologically speaking, it is clear that the growing influence of "administrative consumerism", as well as the idea of "socialisation of risks" caused the evolution. Technically speaking, the enlargement of administrative liability was achieved both by the administrative courts – especially in certain "sensitive" areas such as public hospital liability – and by the legislator, a number of statutes having been passed, mainly since 1980, dealing with the subject of state liability.

Secondly, unlike English law, French law on administrative tortious liability is based upon a general concept of fault. This characteristic is actually common to the whole French law of torts – both private and public. However, in the particular field of administrative law, it simply means that the administrative courts could – and still can – evolve their case law by reference to that general standard of what a "normal" operation of administration should and should not be. The solutions of the courts thus do not have to fit in some strictly delimited "pigeon-holes" like those found in English law. A French administrative court is even free to state that a public authority has committed a fault which leads to its liability – "*une faute de nature à engager sa responsabilité*"- without determining to which kind of fault that belongs.

Thirdly, it is very important to mention that in French administrative law the main kind of fault – indeed, the one most frequently sanctioned in practice – is illegality, and that any illegality is, by its nature, an administrative fault likely to give rise to civil liability if it directly causes damage. The equivalence between illegality and fault also applies to procedural irregularities subject, however, to an important qualification. A procedural irregularity will not lead to liability where it appears that the decision was, in substance, justified; in that situation administrative courts will consider that there is not a sufficient link of causation between the illegality and the damage, since the decision could have been taken in any event.

Fourthly, the main way in which French administrative courts have reduced the ambit of administrative liability is by admitting that, in some fields, such liability should be subject to a condition of gross fault – *faute lourde*. The rationale invoked to justify this special requirement is that the corresponding activities are particularly difficult to perform and that, therefore, simple faults, committed in their operation, have to be forgiven or at least ignored in any legal sense. That such a formula is vague and open-ended cannot, of course, be doubted. What, however, is even clearer is the fact that the list of activities that can engage liability only in the event that the *faute* is *lourde* has shrunk over the years.[25] Thus, nowadays, the list comprises only police activities (provided these are material activities and are not merely related to decision-making), activities related to tax services,[26] and activities which control local government and those public or private institutions which state authorities are legally expected to monitor.

Even though the condition of gross fault is an important limitation in the ambit of administrative liability, it is not the only obstacle that the courts have put in the path of liability. Two others are worth mentioning.

The first derives from the fact that administrative courts are sometimes reluctant to compensate certain categories of damages. Up until 1961,[27] this was the case for mental anguish –

[25] For instance, until recently the list included a case of great practical importance – liability for medical and surgical accidents in public hospitals

[26] Except that since 1990 the requirement of gross fault has been limited to situations in which those services meet special difficulties in the assessment of taxpayers' situations.

[27] Conseil d'Etat, Assemblée, 24 novembre 1961, Letisserand, *Recueil des arrêts du Conseil d'Etat,* 661.

"*douleur morale*"; and it is still the case for damages consisting in future economic losses, which administrative courts frequently refuse to compensate because they do not consider them as sufficiently certain.[28]

The second limitation can be found in the rigorous way in which French administrative courts deal with the problem of causation where the plaintiff has contributed through his own fault to the damage for which he is seeking compensation. Some planning law cases clearly reveal this strictness. Thus, where a developer has, for example, been granted an illegal planning permission and is adversely affected by certain consequences of that illegality – for instance, because he has to pay damages to the neighbours of the developed land – and then acts against the administration, he will generally be confronted with the argument that he, himself, has committed a fault when applying for an illegal permission, and that his fault counterbalances, totally or partially, the fault committed by the administration when granting the unlawful permission.[29]

Until recently another limitation on administrative liability came from the fact that administrative courts were usually very tight-fisted when determining the amount of damages they would award to successful plaintiffs. Certainly, their attitude seemed stricter than that adopted by the ordinary courts when adjudicating on similar issues. This tendency, however, is less apparent today and many commentators would argue that it belongs in the past.[30]

Fourthly, and contrary to what was said above, French administrative law has, since the end of nineteenth century, accepted that in certain circumstances the administration might

[28] That attitude is often visible in cases concerning planning law. For example, a developer who has illegally been refused planning permission and who tries to get compensation for the sales profits or the rents he claims to have lost because of that illegal refusal usually will fail because the judges will not be convinced that the commercialisation would have been beneficial. See Jean-Bernard Auby, *Répertoire Dalloz, Résponsabilité de la puissance publique*, under *Urbanisme*.

[29] See ibid.

[30] See, for example, L Neville Brown and John S Bell, *French Administrative Law* (OUP, 1998), 200.

be liable even though it is guilty of no fault. This is illustrated in two sets of cases.

In the first, the admission of "no-fault" liability stems from the idea of risk: the administration will have to compensate for the damage it has caused even if its behaviour was quite correct because its activity, by its very nature, created risks. A classic example is the accidental injury of a bystander through the use of firearms by the police.[31] Another example of where "no-fault" liability applies is where public works cause, or the presence of a public installation causes, damages to people who are not users but merely neighbours.

The second type of situation in which liability without fault may arise is based upon the idea of breach of equality. The rationale here is that even if the attitude of the administration was not unlawful or negligent, if it has caused a damage which appears to be both "special" and "abnormal" it will be liable. Nowadays, the prevailing view is that it would be unfair – more specifically, contrary to the principle of equality – to leave people who have suffered such damage without compensation. That theory has been applied by the Conseil d'Etat to damages caused by lawful administrative decisions,[32] and even to damages caused by statutes[33] or international treaties ratified by the French State.[34] However, it is worth noting that the practical

[31] Conseil d'Etat, 24 juin 1949, Lecomte et Daramy, *Recueil des arrêts du Conseil d'Etat*, 307.

[32] The main application of that theory concerns cases where the administration refuses the assistance of the police enforcing a judicial decision – expelling, for example, a tenant who does not pay his or her rent because of a threat to public order. The important decision here is Conseil d'Etat, 30 novembre 1923, Couiteas, *Recueil des arrêts du Conseil d'Etat*, 789.

[33] The landmark decision was Conseil d'Etat, Assemblée, 14 janvier 1938, *Société des produits laitiers La Fleurette*, *Recueil des arrêts du Conseil d'Etat*, 25. In that case a statute had been passed which implied the prohibition of a product, which was made only by the La Fleurette company. Notwithstanding the fact that the company obtained compensation, this kind of "legislative" liability is admitted in only a very small number of cases.

[34] As in legislative liability, there are only a few cases in which compensation has been effectively granted. In the first case, in which the principle of liability due to the ratification of a treaty was accepted, the damage was not considered

impact of this heading is limited: the requirement of "special" and "abnormal" damage is an effective filter in contrast to liability without fault which is grounded on the "risk" rationale and which is frequently and successfully invoked.

(c) German law

In German law, tort liability of public bodies is widely discussed. Reform has been considered for over twenty years. Its unquestioned aim is a modern, unified responsibility for wrongs committed by public bodies – mostly, but not entirely, independent of fault, and based on statute. At present, however, most of the law is judge-made; it is secreted in many different kinds of causes of action, and it is not always clear.[35] In this book, however, we will concentrate solely on those situations where damages are sought for breach of an official duty (*Amtspflichtverletzung*) – comparable to the factual situations in our five English cases. This liability of public bodies flows from the combined application[36] of Article 34 of the

as being special: Conseil d'Etat, Assemblée, 30 mars 1966, *Compagnie d'énergie radio-électrique*, *Recueil des arrêts du Conseil d'Etat*, 257. Compensation was, conversely, granted in the case of "*Dame Burgat*" – Conseil d'Etat, Section, 29 octobre 1976, *Recueil des arrêts du Conseil d'Etat*, 452; the claim came from a landowner, whose tenant was a diplomat and who had found it impossible therefore to insist on rent being paid because of the tenant's immunity.

[35] For example: "Expropriation" (*Enteignung*) – Article 14 of the Basic Law; "expropriation-like wrong" (*enteignungsgleicher Eingriff*); "expropriation-like act" (*enteignender Eingriff*); "special sacrifice" (*Aufopferung*); "sacrifice-like wrong" (*aufopferungsgleicher Eingriff*); and others. All these causes of action imply that the public body acts in a public function, not in a solely fiscal matter. In the latter case – as in other, solely financial or private relationships of public entities (e.g., example the protestant churches, universities, state banks (*Bundesbank, Sparkassen*)) – the liability for any wrong will be similar to that of private law entities (BGB, §§ 89, 31 or § 831).

[36] We will be dealing only with the liability of public bodies and not with the liability of their employees. The latter will result from BGB, § 839 only if there is no liability of the public body according to the combined application of Article 34 of the Constitution and BGB, § 839 and only if the employee has the status of a civil servant (*Beamter*). Other employees will be liable in accordance with BGB, §§ 823 *et seq.* where no state liability is envisaged.

Constitution[37] and § 839 of the BGB.[38] This means that public bodies are liable in damages to individuals injured by their own (or their employees') culpable failure to perform properly any official duty owed to the individual. Liability is excluded where, first, the breach of a duty is due to a negligent act only and the individual injured can obtain redress from another source (BGB, § 839 I 2);[39] secondly, where the victim did not make use of any legal remedy which could have mitigated his damages (BGB, § 839 III);[40] and, thirdly, where a statute expressly provides for such an eventuality.[41] Here, it will suffice to draw the

[37] Article 34 states:

"If any person, in the exercise of a public office entrusted to him, violates his official obligations to a third party, liability shall rest in principle on the state or on the public body which employs him. In the event of wilful or grossly negligent conduct, the right of recourse shall be reserved. In respect of claims for compensation and of the right of recourse, the jurisdiction of the ordinary courts must not be excluded."

[38] §839 states:

(1) "If an official wilfully or negligently commits a breach of official duty incumbent upon him as against a third party, he shall compensate the third party for any damage arising therefrom. If only negligence is imputable to the official, he may be held liable only if the injured party is unable to obtain compensation elsewhere.

(2) If an official commits a breach of his official duty in giving judgment in an action, he is not responsible for any damage arising therefrom, unless the breach of duty is punished with a public penalty to be forced by criminal proceedings. This provision does not apply to a breach of duty consisting of refusal or delay in the exercise of the office.

(3) The duty to make compensation does not arise if the injured party has wilfully or negligently omitted to avert the injury by making use of a legal remedy".

[39] For this restriction on state liability and its doubtful and limited effects, see below.

[40] There is another restriction with regard to judicial decisions and the liability of the judge respectively to judicial administration (BGB, § 839II: *Spruchrichterprivileg*), which, however, would carry us outside the ambit of this comparative study.

[41] For example, BNotO (*Bundesnotarordnung*, which is the Federal Law on Notaries), § 19, which provides for the personal liability of the notary public; RBHaftG *Reichsbeamtenhaftungsgesetz* (Law on Liability of Civil Servants), § 5 No. 2, which excludes liability for certain political acts in the diplomatic service;

reader's attention to two elements of the cause of action: "fault" and the fact that "the duty must be owed to the individual plaintiff" and not the public at large.

The requirement of culpability has to be seen against the code's historical background: BGB, § 839 was designed originally to cater solely for the liability of a public official himself.[42] The central idea was that such an official should fear liability in damages only where he is at fault. Individual responsibility is of less significance where the state takes over liability.[43] In the current debates over reforms, German writers remain convinced that the fault requirement should be loosened, but there is considerable disagreement as to the extent that this should happen.[44] These debates should not, however, conceal the fact that the concept of fault in German civil law (in contrast to the concept of fault in criminal law) is already understood in a very broad way.[45] So, as in English law, the standard of care in cases of negligence is an objective one, concentrating on the reasonable person in general and – with regard to particular groups or professions – on the special high standard of care one can expect from such particular group or profession. In practice, the test thus often comes close to the notion of strict liability; and it has

for further discussion, especially on the constitutionality of such restrictions on state liability, see Ossenbühl, *Staatshaftungsrecht* (5th ed., 1996), 79 *et seq.*

[42] The old (Roman law) principle – *si excessit, privatus est* – known also in English law, along with disputes over the legislative competence for state liability rules, induced the draftsmen of the civil code to refrain from any rule on public liability (leaving this issue to the member states), although not from rules on liability of public bodies acting fiscally (see BGB, §§ 89, 31). For further details, see *Entwurf eines Einführungsgesetzes zum BGB für das Deutsche Reich*, 1. *Lesung nebst Motiven* (1888), 185.

[43] First introduced to the whole of Germany by the *Beamtenhaftungsgesetz* of 1 August 1909 (GS 691). This was later acknowledged in Article 131 of the Weimar Constitution 1919.

[44] Compare Pfab, *Staatshaftung in Deutschland* (1997), passim.

[45] For details, see Markesinis, *German Law of Obligations*, Vol. 2, *The Law of Torts, A Comparative Introduction* (3rd ed., 1997); Deutsch, "Der Begriff der Fahrlässigkeit im Zivilrecht" *Jura* 1987, 505.

been demonstrated that in most litigation concerning breach of official duty the issue of fault is rarely an obstacle for plaintiffs.[46]

Secondly, discretionary acts of public bodies (or their employees) are, in Germany, subject to judicial review to a far greater extent than in English law. Thus, a German judge may rule on and find fault even where the official acted within the ambit of his discretion (as will be shown in detail below). The discretionary character of an act is not in principle, therefore, a bar to justiciability; nor does it hinder the proof of careless decision-taking within the ambit of the discretion. The test applied by German courts is much wider than the *Wednesbury*[47] test of reasonableness that prevails in English law.

If the requirement of fault is no real obstacle to state liability the same is not true of the second element, namely "that the duty must be owed to the individual to protect his interests". This serves as an effective filter to remove from all public wrongs those cases where the state itself might be liable in damages. The duty must not exist solely for the benefit of the general public, but must at least also protect the individual or a class to which the individual/plaintiff belongs. The claimant must thus be such a protected individual or a member of a protected group, and the duty must exist to protect especially those interests of the individual that have been injured. The parallels here with the English requirements of liability for breach of statutory duty are evident. Nevertheless, one must remain conscious of the dangers that would accompany any complete assimilation. Although there are many decisions on this issue leading to some uncertainty over the exact application of this requirement in given cases,[48] the approach of German law seems to be stricter

---

[46] *Zur Reform des Staatshaftungsrechts, rechtstatsächliche Erkenntnisse in Staatshaftungssachen, Verwaltungserhebung und Gerichtsauswertung* (1976), edited by the Bundesministerium der Justiz, 34, 202 – only 14.1% of the claims failed because of the absence of fault.

[47] *Associated Provincial Picture Houses* v. *Wednesbury Corp.* [1948] 1 KB 223.

[48] Münchener, *Kommentar/Papier*, BGB (3rd ed., 1997), § 839, n. 227; for proposals to streamline the discussion, see *Ladeur*, "Zur Bestimmung des drittschützenden Charakters von Amtspflichten im Sinne von § 839 BGB und Art. 34 GG – insbesondere bei Aufsichtspflichten" *DÖV* 1994, 665.

than that found in English cases. Thus, where it is open for policy considerations to play a part in the outcome of a dispute, they tend to focus on the relevance and meaning of the official duty and not so much on the wider considerations of justice, fairness and economic efficiency which one finds in English decisions. One, therefore, starts with the premise that fairness and justice require the state to be held liable to the individual for public wrong, except where the official duty is owed only to the public at large. Although the element of "duty towards the individual" (*drittbezogene Amtspflicht*) is phrased as a requirement and not only in a negative form as an obstacle to the claim, the relation of rule and exception in English and German law seems to be the reverse.[49] This may be illustrated by contrasting the indicators of such "duty towards the individual" with the requirements of state liability in English law laid down by Lord Browne-Wilkinson in the *Bedfordshire* case (see below).

It is well established that there is a "duty towards the individual" when the (particular) individual has a right to claim performance of that duty (*öffentlich-rechtlicher Erfüllungsanspruch*). Claim of and duty towards the individual are two sides of the same coin. For example, an applicant may claim the issue of a building permission where he has complied with certain requirements. If the permission is not issued, or is issued too late, or is (illegally) made subject to a supplementary condition, a private law cause of action will arise.[50] Of course, these situations are

[49] This is obvious in the decision of the Federal Court of Justice with regard to the banking control system, where the court inferred from the silence of the statutory rule that the duty was owed towards the individual: BGH of 15 February 1979, BGHZ 74, 144, 147 = NJW 1979, 1354; BGH of 12 July 1979, BGHZ 75, 120, 122 = NJW 1979, 1879. For doubts on the constitutionality of the amendments of the statute (Kreditwesengesetz, as amended on 20 December 1984), see Münchener, *Kommentar/Papier*, above at n. 48, § 839, n. 250, 251.

[50] BGH of 14 December 1978, NJW 1979, 641, 642; BGH of 10 March 1994, NJW 1994, 1647; BGH of 13 July 1989, NJW 1990, 505 (marriage officer arriving too late in the hospital for the marriage ceremony, one fiancée having died already); compare also BGH of 6 May 1993, NJW 1993, 2303, 2304; BGH of 24 February 1994, NJW 1994, 2091; Münchener *Kommentar/Papier*, § 839, n. 228; *Wurm*, JA 1992, 1, 2.

less problematic and do not arise frequently in practice because the individual may usually launch an appeal against the decision and thereby obtain what he or she is entitled to claim. Although not identical, this class of case comes close to those situations in English law where Lord Browne Wilkinson referred to breaches of statutory duty *simpliciter*.[51]

Another instance giving rise to a duty towards an individual is where the public body and the individual have entered into a special relationship. The duties of protection and care arising from such relationship are owed to the individual, and also to third parties included in the realm of protection (*Schutzwirkung zugunsten Dritter*).[52] For example, a school owes a special duty of care towards its pupils.[53] In addition, a school has the duty to prevent pupils from causing harm to others. Thus, if a pupil damages the car of X during a school excursion, the responsible body may be liable towards the car owner.[54] It is tempting here to draw parallels with the *Dorset Yacht* case, although one might also be inclined to compare this element of the "duty towards the individual" with the requirement of proximity found in the

[51] *X (Minors)* v. *Bedfordshire County Council* [1995] 3 WLR 165, 166.

[52] BGH of 20 June 1974, NJW 1974, 1816, 1817 – a slaughterhouse owed a duty towards the employee of the butcher, who had to use the slaughter house; this notion of third party protection is known not only in tort law but especially in contract law, where contractual duties may involve the protection of persons close to the parties. For further discussion of contracts which protect third parties, see Markesinis, Lorenz, Dannemann, *German Law of Obligations*, Vol. I, *Law of Contracts and Restitution, A Comparative Introduction* (OUP, 1997), 276.

[53] BGH of 27 April 1981, NJW 1982, 37, 38; BGH of 10 March 1983, FamRZ 1984, 1211 (both concerning the negligent control of a school bus stop). In most cases there will be no liability of the school and its responsible body because damage will be covered by insurance against school accidents taken out by the schools. This exception will not apply, however, when violations of the right of personality (*Persönlichkeitsrechtsverletzungen*) are at issue and money compensation for pain and suffering sought: OLG Zweibrücken of 6 May 1997, NJW 1998, 995: the responsible body had to pay DM 1.600, to a pupil who had consistently been made fun of by his teacher in front of the class causing the pupil great psychological harm.

[54] LG Hamburg of 26 April 1991, NJW 1992, 377; in that case a cause of action against the pupil himself would have been unsuccessful due primarily to his lack of means.

Caparo test.[55] There are also differences, however, insofar as, in general, the required proximity need not exist between the tort-feasor and the injured person but between the injured person and the person protected by a special relationship with the tort-feasor. In addition, this duty has been extended – in contrast to contract law – towards those individuals who come into contact with the person protected: the duty of the public body encompasses the duty to prevent harm from the entrusted person as well as to prevent that person from doing harm to others. Thus, the scope of the duty is much broader than the duty of care considered in the *Dorset Yacht case*.

A "duty towards the individual" will also arise where the public body directly infringes absolute rights of an individual, namely his life, body, health, freedom, property (and other rights or interests of comparable weight, for example the right of personality), but not his purely economic interests.[56]

If none of these indicators are present, a "duty towards the individual" may arise under the protective purpose of the rule (*Schutzzweck der Norm*[57]); the rule – which imposes a certain duty on the public body – must have been created, inter alia, to prevent the mischief that occurred. But this need not necessarily follow from the express intention of the legislator; it suffices that such protection for the individual arises from the nature of public dealings and the circumstances of such dealings, even if the rule has been laid down primarily for the protection of the public in general. One indicator of the protective purpose of the duty is the availability of a public law remedy for an injured per-

[55] *Caparo-Industries Plc* v. *Dickman* [1990] 2 AC 605.

[56] BGH of 1 February 1982, NJW 1983, 627, 628; Münchener *Kommentar/Papier*, § 839, n. 229.

[57] The theory was first adopted in relation to breaches of contractual duties, and was later accepted in the law of torts with regard to liability under BGB, §823; originally, it modified the concept of causation in BGB § 823 I, and, subsequently, it influenced the definition of the "protective norm" (*Schutzgesetz*) in the sense of BGB, §823 II (compare Markesinis, above at n. 52, Vol. II, *The Law of Torts*, 101), and the application of BGB, § 839 (compare Canaris, Schutzgesetze – Verkehrspflichten – Schutzpflichten, in *Festschrift Larenz* (1983), 30, 40.

son; another indicator is the special danger for the life and health of an individual resulting from these dealings. If public dealings create a special situation where an individual can rely on the duty of care owed to him by a public body, this indicates that duties arising from public dealings also have the purpose of protecting individuals; but the extent of the protective purpose may be limited to certain goods, especially to absolute rights and interests.[58] This is especially the case, for example, with regard to the duty to ensure safe traffic on the roads (*Straßenverkehrssicherungspflicht*), which duty exists towards every individual road-user,[59] but only with regard to life, body, health, liberty, property and other rights and interests of comparable weight; the duty does not extend to protection against economic loss.[60] Thus, if traffic lights are installed wrongly and, as a result, an accident occurs which causes injury to individuals and damage to property, the public authority will be liable for all these damages. However if, due to the wrong installation of traffic lights, a traffic congestion occurs, no liability will arise towards individuals who suffered economic loss because they were caught in the resulting traffic jam.

If there is a duty towards the (respective) individual,[61] and the protected rights and interests of the individual have been injured, there will be no further room for policy arguments and the state will be held liable – provided, of course, that the other requirements mentioned above are fulfilled.

[58] BGH of 26 January 1989, BGHZ 106, 323 = NJW 1989, 976 – Altlasten, i.e., planning and contamination of soil.

[59] The German cases differ considerably from the English cases, as exemplified by *Ancell* v. *McDermott* [1993] 4 All ER 355.

[60] BGH of 18 December 1972, NJW 1973, 463.

[61] No duty towards the individual, however, exists with respect to legislative acts, such as the failure to provide necessary laws or the violation of individual rights by virtue of unjust or improper laws. Legislative acts – in comparison to specific acts towards individuals or groups of persons – are owed only to the public in general and, thus, cannot constitute a duty towards an individual or a violation of an individual's rights, unless specified by administrative or judicial acts. Other principles, however, apply with regard to "legislative wrongs" under European law; see Joined Cases C-6 and 9/90 *Francovich* v. *Italy* [1991] ECR I-5357.

4. Five factual situations

(a) English law

The facts and legal issues raised by our five English cases are so well known that we could have dispensed with the need of stating them again. Nevertheless, we do so in bare outline, mainly in order to facilitate their comparative juxtaposition with the French and German cases the facts of which are given in subsections (b) and (c) below.

First, *Hill* v. *Chief Constable of West Yorkshire*[62] involved a claim by the mother of a deceased woman (suing for damages to her estate) against the police on the grounds that because of their (alleged) negligence they failed, during their investigations of the commission of a series of similar crimes, to apprehend their perpetrator. This failure allowed the criminal to remain at large for a further period of time during which he murdered the plaintiff's daughter. The action failed.

Secondly, *X (Minors)* v. *Bedfordshire County Council*[63] was one of two "child-abuse" actions (consolidated and heard together with three other cases not discussed in this book). It arose in connection with a claim that a local authority negligently and in breach of its statutory obligations failed to exercise its powers to institute care proceedings after it has received serious reports that the plaintiff/child had been the subject of parental abuse and neglect. The second case – *M (A Minor)* v. *Newham London Borough Council* – was the mirror image of the first, since it involved a claim for negligently removing the child from maternal care on the basis of an unfounded belief that the abuse had taken place by the mother's cohabitee and the conclusion that the mother was unable to protect her child.

The third case, *Elguzouli-Daff* v. *Commissioner of Police of the Metropolis*,[64] involved the Crown Prosecution Service. Torts actions were brought by two persons who were detained in cus-

---

[62] [1988] 1 WLR 1049.
[63] [1995] 3 WLR 152.
[64] [1995] 2 WLR 173.

tody for suspected crimes. After a long periods in detention – 22 and 85 days respectively – the Crown Prosecution Service (CPS) discontinued proceedings against them on the grounds that there was insufficient evidence. The plaintiffs' statement of claim against the CPS was struck out by the judge who held that they disclosed no reasonable cause of action. The Court of Appeal unanimously rejected the plaintiffs' appeal, on the ground that the CPS owed no duty of care to those it was prosecuting.

The chronologically fourth example can be found in *Stovin* v. *Wise*.[65] In that case a local authority failed to exercise its statutory power to direct a private landowner, on whose property lay an obstruction, to have it removed in order to improve visibility at a nearby road junction which was known to have caused traffic accidents in the past. The plaintiff, who was injured at this junction by the defendant's car, claimed damages against him for his injuries. The defendant, in turn, joined the council as a third party. The action against the defendant having been settled, the battle shifted to the council's potential liability. By a majority of three to two, the House of Lords ruled in favour of the council.

The final case is *W* v. *Essex County Council*.[66] Here, parents and their children brought an action against a local authority, which placed in their foster care a child who was known to be a sexual abuser. An action by the molested children against the local authority succeeded by majority; but the parents' action for nervous shock was dismissed.

(b) French law

Hill v. *Chief Constable of West Yorkshire*. No exact equivalent of *Hill* was found in French published case law. However, this does not mean that a failure by the police to react to certain situations where action was needed cannot lead to public liability. For

---

[65] [1996] 3 WLR 388.

[66] [1998] 3 WLR 534. At the time of writing, the case is listed for a House of Lords hearing, but we have not been given a date.

example, in the case of *Ville de Perpignan*,[67] the municipality was held liable because the local police had been warned that a cinema show was about to take place in premises that were not safe for fire purposes. Fire broke out on the premises and the plaintiff was injured. His action for damages against the police succeeded.

The case of *Mme Garagnon*[68] can also be mentioned here. In that case, after a French woman and her Algerian husband divorced, the husband succeeded in taking their children to Algeria. This was contrary to a decision by the Minister of the Interior that had prohibited them being taken outside the French territory. The state was held liable to Mme Garagnon, the Conseil d'Etat accepting that the airport police, had they checked the relevant file properly, would have realised that the father was prohibited from taking the children outside the French jurisdiction.

In such cases, when public liability is accepted, it is because the omission by the police to do what they should have done is considered to amount to such a serious wrongdoing that it amounts to gross fault (*faute lourde*). Indeed, as we have already made clear, police activities are one of the fields in which the condition of gross fault is required before public liability can be admitted.[69]

The above cases illustrate that where the omission by the police is not serious enough to be considered as a gross fault the administration will not be held liable. An example of this can be found in *Société Le Profil*.[70] During a hold-up by robbers, the policemen charged with protecting money which was being transported failed to react when they should have. The lateness and the inefficiency of their intervention were not considered as constituting a gross fault, and the company, whose money was transported and stolen, could not obtain compensation for its loss.

[67] Conseil d'Etat, 29 juillet 1948, *Recueil des arrêts du Conseil d'Etat*, 213

[68] Conseil d'Etat, 26 juin 1985, *Recueil des arrêts du Conseil d'Etat*, 254

[69] At least, as was mentioned above, where material, "physical" activities are concerned. Where what is criticised is an illegal decision, liability is subject only to a condition of simple fault.

[70] Conseil d'Etat, 27 avril 1979, *Recueil des arrêts du Conseil d'Etat*, 171.

One must conclude the above comments by returning to a point already made concerning the fluid nature of the principle of *faute lourde*. The few examples given above suggest that whereas the principle could be used as a device limiting the police's eventual liability, the dividing line between ordinary and grave fault is neither obvious nor great. At any rate, this is likely to be the reaction of an English lawyer in cases such as the above, for whom the concept's fluidity will appear more a potential source of uncertainty – which, in the last resort, can be resolved only by litigation – than an effective limitation device. Even if that is so, however, the potential liability rule does not seem to have caused any economic or practical problems for the French police.

X v. *Bedfordshire County Council and M* v. *Newham London Borough Council*. There appears to be only one published case in which social services were held liable because of their negligence in the exercise of the powers vested in them for the purposes of protecting children in danger of family abuse. (This administrative duty is called *protection maternelle et infantile*.) In *Epoux Ouaras*[71] a three-year-old girl had been sent, with the agreement of her parents, to stay with a foster family for three months. The foster family, which was not French, had been selected by an association devoted to children care. The child was seriously maltreated. Her parents were granted compensation. The Conseil d'Etat considered that the administration was at fault for not having verified the reliability of the foster family carefully.

Another case offers a possible comparison with *Newham*. In *M et Mme Pillon*[72] – the Conseil d'Etat held that a social service had committed no fault in not warning the authority able to institute care proceedings about the threat posed to the health of children entrusted in the care of a particular family. (Information collected by the agency pointed to such dangers, and the concern should have been even greater given that the family had refused permission to the social workers to enter their

[71] Conseil d'Etat, 23 septembre 1987, *Recueil des arrêts du Conseil d'Etat*, 290.
[72] Conseil d'Etat, 4 mai 1983, no.22811.

house and talk to the children.). To an English lawyer these facts would indicate the presence of fault, but we cannot labour this point too much given that the finding of fault depended on the facts in each case, and we do not have them before us as the court did. The outcome of the litigation could be seen as an illustration of how the controlling device of fault works in practice. However, one must also note the dangers that may arise from the fact that such determinations may only be possible *after* litigation has taken place. To an English lawyer this observation will not just be crucial, but also, arguably, a reinforcement for his view to dispose such disputes without the cost and delays of a full trial. Nevertheless, one must also repeat – perhaps with some degree of surprise – the paucity of litigated examples, something which must indicate that in *practice* the potential liability rule has not opened the floodgates of litigation.

Elguzouli-Daff v. *Commissioner of Police of the Metropolis.* In French law, the question of state liability to people who have been improperly detained before trial has, since 1970, been governed by statutory rules. Thus, a statute passed on 17 July 1970 gives persons who, after having been detained in custody, are not subsequently sentenced, the right to compensation. This right is not subject to proving the presence of any fault. Until 1996 it was subject to the condition that the damage was "manifestly abnormal and particularly serious"; this condition, however, was removed by a 1996 Act.[73] Thus, nowadays, on the basis of this legislation, about half of the people who claim compensation receive it every year. The average amount of the compensation is 63,000 francs – about £6,300 per claim.[74] The amount, once again, covers "moral damages" and a separate (and additional) claim can be made for provable economic losses.

Stovin v. *Wise.* No exact equivalent to *Stovin* v. *Wise* can be found in the published French case law. The problem which arose in that case could, however, be resolved by French law, since in the Road Code (*Code de la voirie routière*), article L.114-

---

[73] Loi du 30 décembre 1996 relative a la détention provisoire.

[74] René Chapus, *Droit administratif général* (12th ed., 1998), no.1481.

1 we find provisions which entitle public authorities to take the kind of decision which was not taken in the *Stovin* case. The powers thereby given to the appropriate authorities belong to what French administrative law calls administrative police (*police administrative*) an area of the law in which, as was mentioned above, public liability is subject to a condition of gross fault (*faute lourde*). Thus, the administration could be held liable if it could be shown that it had failed to direct a landowner to remove an obstruction in a situation in which such action was necessary.

There are two cases with which *Stovin* might, nonetheless, be compared. Both cases concerned circumstances in which what was criticised was the omission by the administration to use powers concerning road traffic, but both of which related to private properties (more precisely, private roads which were open to the public). Thus, in the first case, *Commune de Maisons-Laffitte*, the *Conseil d'Etat* stated that the local authority had committed a gross fault, leading to its liability, because it had failed to make sure that various obstacles and barriers had been properly visible through appropriate lighting.[75] In the second case, *Ville de Paris c. Marabout*,[76] the local authority was equally condemned for having neglected to act against illegal car-parking in a private road which was open to the public, but where parking was forbidden by a regulation issued by the same local authority. M Marabout, who lived at the bottom of the road and who was deprived of a normal access to his property, was thus granted compensation.

W v. *Essex County Council.* The most recent cases concerning damages caused by children in foster care concerned damages suffered, not by the foster family, but by third persons. In one case decided in 1998 by the Administrative Court of Appeal of Bordeaux[77] (*Consorts Fraticola*) a seventeen-year-old adolescent,

[75] Conseil d'Etat, 8 mai 1963, Commune de Maisons-Laffitte, *Droit administratif*, 1963, no.215.

[76] Conseil d'Etat, Assemblée, 20 octobre 1972, Ville de Paris c. Marabout, *Actualité Juridique Droit Administratif*, novembre 1972, 597.

[77] C. adm. Bordeaux, 2 février 1998, Consorts Fraticola, Les Petites Affiches, 12 août 98, 3, concl. D. Peano.

while staying with a foster family, killed another youngster during a fight at the local fair. The Administrative Court of Appeal granted total compensation *to the family* of the latter child of approximately 160,000 francs or the approximate equivalent of £16,000. The amount may be considered small, but an English lawyer might well reflect on the fact that in his own system their could be no fatal accidents claim whatsoever, the only amount of damages claimable being by the estate of the victim himself.

What has to be specified is that the Administrative Court of Appeal reached its conclusion by admitting that, in this kind of cases, a presumption of fault would apply. In that case, this meant that the plaintiffs did not have to demonstrate that a fault had been committed, either by the administration in the choice of the foster parents, or by the foster parents in the way they looked after the foster child.[78] On the contrary, it was up to the administration to demonstrate that its behaviour, and the behaviour of the parents, was correct. This it failed to do.

Although there is no recent case concerning this issue, it is probable that administrative liability for the damages suffered by the foster family itself, and not by third persons, is even wider. It is probably a liability without fault, this kind of regime being one, which usually benefits all people harmed when acting in the public service.[79] One cannot be certain of this conclusion, however, since in older cases the Conseil d'Etat imposed liability only in cases of proven fault.[80] Even this result, however, would make French law different from English law since in the *Essex* case – and for a variety of reasons, which we shall examine further down – liability to the parents was denied.

[78] The same presumption of fault had in fact been previously accepted by the Conseil d'Etat in one particular situation where damages are caused by children whose parents are dead or who have been abandoned by their parents, and who are under state protection (*pupilles de l'Etat*): Conseil d'Etat, 19 octobre 1990, Ingremeau, *Revue de droit public*, 1990–1866, concl. C de la Verpillière.

[79] See *Répertoire Dalloz de la résponsabilité de la puissance publique*, V° Collaborateurs occasionnels.

[80] Conseil d'Etat, 30 mars 1935, Derue, *Recueil des arrêts du Conseil d'Etat*, 132 – 30 mars 1938, Derue, *Recueil des arrêts du Conseil d'Etat*, 332 – 11 décembre 1957, Dle Champel, *Recueil des arrêts du Conseil d'Etat*, 1022.

It must finally be mentioned that, if the child in foster care was a juvenile delinquent – more often staying in centres, but sometimes placed with families – the damages that he or she would cause would have to be compensated on the ground of liability without fault,[81] whoever the plaintiff was – a member of the foster family or a third person.

(c) German law

Comparable to *Hill* v. *Chief Constable of West Yorkshire* is a German case[82] in which the plaintiff sued the state claiming damages because the police did not act to prevent a robbery even though they knew that X and Y, who perpetrated the robbery, were members of a band of robbers and were on the prowl. X and Y later broke into the plaintiff's house. The plaintiff's action against the police was successful.

Secondly, although an exact parallel to the first case in *X (Minors)* v. *Bedfordshire County Council* can be found only in criminal law,[83] the questions of law raised in the second case (*Newham*[84]) are comparable to those considered by a decision of the Court of Appeal of Hamm in 1996.[85] In that case a minor had asked the local youth welfare authority to take care of her because she was experiencing considerable difficulties with her mother and did not wish to live with her any longer. The authority heard the minor and the mother and then applied to the family court, which assigned the right to determine the minor's whereabouts to the authority. The authority sent the minor to a home for children where the minor stayed for about ten months

[81] Conseil d'Etat, Section, 3 février 1956, Thouzellier, Dalloz, 1956–597, note J.M. Auby.

[82] BGH 30 April 1953 LM (Lindenmayer/Möhring = collection of Reported cases), § 839 [Fg] BGB, no 5.

[83] OLG Oldenburg of 2 September 1996, ZfJ 1997, 95. See also OLG Stuttgart of 28 May 1998, NJW 1998, 3131, 3133, also a criminal case, where the social worker was held responsible for acting in a timely and diligent manner to prevent mistreatment of a child who, however, died from this mistreatment!

[84] *M (A minor)* v. *Newham London Borough Council* [1995] 3 WLR 152.

[85] OLG Hamm of 20 November 1996, ZfJ 1997, 433.

before she returned to her mother. The mother sued the state for damages because she was deprived of her daughter through the alleged wrong acts of the youth welfare authority. She maintained that the youth authority should have attempted reconciliation before separating her from her child and, more seriously, that it had also influenced her daughter' s statement before the family court. Evidence was taken and the case went to a full hearing. The claim ultimately failed, but only because the authority was not found to have acted negligently.

Elguzouli-Daff v. *Commssioner of Police of the Metropolis* may be contrasted to a German case decided by the Federal Court of Justice in 1997.[86] The plaintiff had been arrested on charge of fraudulent conversion (March 1990). The state prosecutor had applied to the court for a warrant for arrest, which was granted on condition that the detention should be suspended. The state prosecutor successfully appealed and the plaintiff was kept in detention for several more weeks until the arrest order was suspended in May 1990 and, finally, quashed in November 1990. The criminal proceedings against the plaintiff were stayed in March 1991. The plaintiff claimed damages for false imprisonment. He alleged that both the prosecution and the arrest had been instituted without reasonable or probable cause given that at the time of his arrest it had already become obvious that the incriminating evidence of two witnesses could not be relied upon in the case against him. The court awarded the plaintiff damages for both his material and immaterial loss.

The facts in a decision of the Federal Court of Justice in 1980 come close to those *Stovin* v. *Wise*. A traffic accident happened because the visibility of a road junction was obstructed by a hedge separating the two carriageways. The council argued that its duty was merely to ensure safe conditions on the road and that it did not extend towards the plaintiff who should have taken more care. The argument was considered and rejected. The court granted damages to the plaintiff.[87]

[86] BGH of 16 October 1997, NJW 1998, 751.
[87] BGH NJW 1980, 2194.

In the final case, comparable to *W* v. *Essex County Council*, the local youth welfare authority placed a child for adoption with the plaintiffs. The plaintiffs had made clear that they wanted to adopt only a healthy child. In fact, the child was mentally retarded which the authority could have known had it acted diligently. The plaintiffs successfully claimed damages with regard to their support obligation towards the retarded child.[88]

---

[88] OLG Hamm, FamRZ 1993, 704.

2
How Different Courts have Handled these Cases

1. The reasons given by the English courts for denying liability in negligence

(a) Legalistic reasons: duty, proximity, fairness, justice and reasonableness

We describe these as "legalistic" rather than legal reasons since, in our view, the concepts used to achieve the results are value-neutral on their surface only. Thus, as a rich case law amply demonstrates, all these concepts are fluid enough to justify whatever result the judge has decided to reach before turning to the question of how he should justify his conclusion to the general public. Our tort books are, of course, replete with examples showing how courts use these malleable concepts. In our five illustrations, however, the most recent judicial decisions have demonstrated fairly clearly that the concepts used are only legal smokescreens for a heavy dose of judicial social engineering. We reinforce our assertion that these concepts are, essentially, a smokescreen for disguising value judgments by referring our readers to some interesting extra-judicial utterances on this subject from Lord Mustill.[1] Our assertion that the judgments have

---

[1] "What do courts do?" (1995–96) 3 *Särtryck ur Juridisk Tidskrift*, 611, 620:

"One cannot always be sure, as regards an individual judge, that the reasons published in a judgment are in fact his reasons for the decision. They may have been considered after the event to reconcile the decision with legal materials which appeared to stand in its way, and which played no part in his formation of the conclusion, or to call support from favourable materials for a decision arrived at without recourse to them (for example a decision made intuitively, or on grounds of policy)."

recourse to legal smokescreens does not, however, mean that we prefer the concealment of the true policy reasons which explain (if not justify) these decisions. On the contrary, we welcome this open discussion of policy even if we advocate its refinement and disagree with the results which its application, apparently, dictates. In our view, the current state of affairs which, on the whole, we find unconvincing, will never change, let alone improve, if we fail to test openly the validity of the policy arguments which have been advanced to support the current, restrictive case law. In this context, therefore, we note with satisfaction that as one moves from *Hill* v. *Chief Constable of West Yorkshire*[2] to the most recent cases one detects a greater willingness to justify the results by reference to the policy reasons found mainly in *X (Minors)* v. *Bedfordshire County Council*[3] and, to a lesser extent, *Stovin* v. *Wise*.[4] On the other hand, we also voice some concerns about the non-scientific way in which the policy-oriented debate is taking place since we do not believe that policy arguments can be put forward largely on the strength of hunches rather than verifiable evidence. A refinement of this trend is thus called for if it is to survive in the future. We hope both take place.

The *Hill* decision, which we have taken as the starting point of the current restrictive trend, is, from the "justification" point of view, still in orthodox company. The bulk of the judgments is devoted to the discussion of the usual ingredients of the notion of duty of care. Thus, there is talk of: no liability because of "no duty";[5] no proximity (thus distinguishing it from the *Dorset Yacht* decision);[6] foreseeability, alone, will not suffice for the imposition of liability;[7] no liability for the acts of third parties

---

[2] [1988] 1 WLR 1049.

[3] [1995] 3 WLR 152.

[4] [1996] 3 WLR 388.

[5] [1987] 2 WLR 1126, 1143, per Fox LJ; 1139B, per Glidewell LJ.

[6] Ibid., 1135 E–F, per Fox LJ; *Hill* v. *Chief Constable of West Yorkshire* [1988] 1 WLR 1049, 1053A, 1955, per Lord Keith.

[7] [1987] 2 WLR 1126, 1134E, per Fox LJ; *Hill* v. *Chief Constable of West Yorkshire* [1988] 1 WLR 1049, 1052I, per Lord Keith.

(who are neither servants or agents);[8] absence of special relationship between plaintiff and defendant;[9] and, finally, whether the imposition of liability would be "fair, just and reasonable".[10] Notably (and surprisingly) absent from this list of "technical" arguments is the fact that *Hill* involved an omission instead of a bad act. As we shall note below, this point which, arguably, could have on its own disposed of the *Hill* claim, emerged in a key way in the judgments of both the majority and the dissent in the *Stovin* case. It has been argued, not entirely unconvincingly, that the policy justifications given for the *Hill* result (and discussed below) may form part of *obiter dicta* and not an integral part of the *ratio decidendi* of the decision.[11]

In the *Bedfordshire* decision, which is our second focal point, the "technical", legal arguments connected with tort liability were limited to the enquiry whether the local authority owed a direct duty of care. Lord Browne-Wilkinson's remarks are brief on two of the usual requirements – foreseeability and proximity – largely because the local authority (wisely) chose not to challenge the fact that they were satisfied. Instead, he asserted (without discussion[12] and, some might argue, not so convincingly)

[8] [1987] 2 WLR 1126, 1133E, per Fox LJ; 1139 G per Glidewell LJ.

[9] Ibid., 1130 G, per Fox LJ; 1139F, per Glidewell LJ. *Osman* v. *Ferguson* [1993] 4 All ER 344, discussed below in Chapter Three, was one of the exceptional cases where a special relationship was held to have arisen between the police and the plaintiff/tortfeasor's victim. Nonetheless, the action failed.

[10] [1987] 2 WLR 1126, 1136 H, per Fox LJ; 1139H, per Glidewell LJ.

[11] Tregilgas-Davey, "*Osman* v. *Metropolitan Police Commissioner: The Cost of Police Protectionism*" (1993) 56 *MLR* 732, 737.

[12] [1995] 3 WLR 152 at 183. This was, indeed, accepted by the majority in *Marc Rich & Co. AG* v. *Bishop Rock Marine Co. Ltd.* [1996] 1 AC 211 – a case involving property damage. Two years later an attempt was made to transport this reasoning to cases of physical injury in *Perret* v. *Collins* [1998] 2 Lloyd's Rep. 255 but it was boldly repulsed by a unanimous Court of Appeal. Lord Justice Hobhouse (as he then was) had this to say (at 258) on this crucial issue:

"What the second and third defendants seek to achieve in this case is to extend decisions upon 'economic' loss to cases of personal injury. It represents a fundamental attack upon the principle of tortious liability for negligent conduct, which had caused foreseeable personal injury to others. That such a point should be considered to be even arguable shows how far some of the that the requirement of "fair, just and reasonable", essentially introduced into our system by the *Peabody*[13] and *Caparo*[14] judgments, also applied to cases involving physical harm to the person. He then switched to the policy arguments, which in his view negated the presence of any duty. To these we shall return in greater detail in the next subsection since they represent both in substance and in form one of the most interesting innovations of the judgment.

The *Elguzouli* judgment[15] is notable for the almost complete absence of any discussion of the usual ingredients of the notion of duty of care. Thus, there is only a fleeting reference to "foreseeability"[16] and an unquestioned acceptance of the point already found in Lord Browne-Wilkinson's judgment that the *Caparo* requirement of "fair, just and reasonable" also applies to all cases of negligence liability. One technical argument, however, seems to have escaped Lord Justice Steyn's (as he then was) attention: *Elguzouli*, unlike *Hill* – which plays a pivotal role in Lord Justice Steyn's judgment – was not a case of omission but a case of (distinctly) negligent acts. Yet the policy arguments in favour of immunity were so obviously in the forefront of Lord Justice Steyn's mind that he not only cited *Hill* as providing an

fundamental principles of the law of negligence have come to eroded. The arguments advanced in this case [*viz*. that the kind of wider policy considerations used in *Marc Rich* to justify the majority decision should also be used in this case and absolve the defendants from all liability] illustrate the dangers of substituting for clear criteria, criteria which are incapable of precise definition and involve what can only be described as an element of subjective assessment by the Court; such ultimately subjective assessments tend inevitably to lead to uncertainty and anomaly which can be avoided by a more principled approach."

[13] *Governors of the Peabody Donation Fund* v. *Sir Lindsay Parkinson & Co. Ltd.* [1985] AC 210, 241C, per Lord Keith. The idea can, however, be traced back to Lord Morris' judgment in the *Dorset Yacht* case in 1970.

[14] *Caparo Industries Plc* v *Dickman* [1990] 2 AC 605.

[15] *Elguzoli-Daff* v. *Commissioner of Police of the Metropolis* [1995] 2 WLR 173, 179. Including the judgment of the deputy High Court judge which Lord Justice Steyn (as he then was) described (approvingly) as "robust".

[16] At 183, which the judge was willing to accept as being satisfied.

"instructive analogy",[17] but went even further in asserting that in *Elguzouli* the reasons for immunity were here even stronger. The decision thus provides an even clearer illustration of the current (post-*Anns*[18] and, certainly, post-*Bedfordshire* and *Stovin*) trend to resolve these disputes by an open *if not exclusive* appeal to policy.

The majority and dissenting judgments in *Stovin* are a gold mine of ideas and analysis. Most are related to the issue of tortious liability for breach of statutory rules; and, if combined with the *Bedfordshire* decision must signal a definite move away from the days of *Anns* towards a very restrictive[19] regime of tort liability of public bodies. The majority clearly suggests that nowadays a court which is confronted with such matters is not only obliged to investigate whether the decision in question is justiciable (the policy/operation dichotomy increasingly going out of fashion) but also whether it was irrational in the *Wednesbury*[20] sense (i.e., so unreasonable that no public body could have taken it). Even if it is, a private law claim in damages will not arise unless the court comes to the conclusion that it is "fair, just and reasonable" to make such an award. In this respect, discovering (or inventing) the "policy" of the statute with regard to compensation will be crucial.

Purely from the point of view of the tort of negligence, *Stovin* presents two particular points of interest: first, its prolonged discussion of the distinction between acts and omissions, which as we have already noted received little attention in the *Hill* cases and its successors; secondly, its adoption of the view – which one could argue slipped into the general law of negligence almost without discussion until the House of Lords accepted it

[17] At 181.

[18] *Anns* v *Merton LBC* [1978] AC 728.

[19] It is too early to predict whether *Barrett* v. *Enfield London Borough Council* [1999] 3 WLR 79 can, on its own, reverse this trend. Our own guess, amplified further down, is that *Barrett* will be used technically and cautiously. Thus, if a real change is to come about, it will be through European influences, acknowledged or concealed but, nonetheless, there. See also below at n oo.

[20] *Associated Provincial Picture Houses* v. *Wednesbury Corporation* [1948] 1 KB 223.

in a (fairly) recent and controversial majority decision[21] – that "fair, just and reasonable" is a requirement that is also relevant to all types of harm and not just pure economic loss. Potentially, this represents a significant move towards restricting the ambit of the tort of negligence and is in keeping with other recent attempts[22] to confine the reach of tort law.

Such an ebb and flow of ideas about the exact boundaries of tort liability is not, of course, anything new. On the contrary, the whole history of tort law can be seen as a constant struggle between the rights of the injured versus the rights of their injurers. But these trends do justify two immediate reactions. Thus, first, they render dubious assertions that the tort of negligence is galloping out of control.[23] Its expansive tendencies are at the expense of other torts – *Rylands*, nuisance, to some degree defamation – not its traditional defendants. Secondly, and more relevant to our work, it cannot justify any conclusion that this trend is irreversible. As sure as day will follow night, the current judicial thesis will, itself, give way to a new antithesis and should not thus be seen as anything more than a passing phase in the unending battle to find a workable compromise between these antithetic positions. However, it is also interesting to note that the current position is being achieved through the deployment of the "fair, just and reasonable" device which (a) was first introduced[24] in the context of cases dealing with pure economic loss and (b) was not – originally at any rate – seen as having the potential of overtaking so completely the normative effect of the other ingredients of duty, namely foreseeability and proximity.

The durability of these changes in judicial philosophy will, we think, depend on two prime factors: first, on how convincing the policy reasons nowadays are openly invoked to explain why a

[21] *Marc Rich & Co. AG* v. *Bishop Rock Marines Co. Ltd.* [1995] 3 WLR 227.

[22] *White* v. *Chief Constable of South Yorkshire* [1998] 3 WLR 1510 (psychiatric injury).

[23] Weir, "The Staggering March of Negligence" in Peter Cane and Jane Stapleton (eds), *The Law of Obligations. Essays in Celebration of John Fleming* (OUP, 1998), 97 *ff*.

[24] Subject to the point made earlier that one might be able to trace this idea in *one* of the judgments in the *Dorset Yacht* case.

particular result is (or is not) fair, just and reasonable; and, secondly, upon whether it will, in the long run, prove politically acceptable to introduce such extensive immunities in an (almost) blanket manner. Decisions like the one handed down in the *Essex County Council* case – our last focal point – may well bring more into relief not only the difficulty of applying wide *dicta* coming from "striking out" cases, but also the essential unfairness of the current trends which, it could be said, sacrifice justice so completely to the altar of financial good management. We must thus move on to examine the policy reasons given for these results and then superimpose a new influence, which has not yet been felt by our law: the human rights aspect of these extreme decisions. In our view, it is this kind of approach that is likely to reveal the unproved assumptions of the current conservative judicial trends. They will be shown to be even weaker when tested against the solutions adopted by some other legal systems which share the same economic and social characteristics as our own.

(b) Policy reasons

One should start by reminding the reader that in many of these cases – certainly the most recent vintage – liability was denied mainly by invoking the public law statutory duty/powers arguments mentioned earlier. But in some decisions a number of unproved and, perhaps, unprovable policy propositions were also used – in some instances, such as in *Stovin*, "thrown in" at the end – in order to support the view that it was not fair, just and reasonable to find a duty of care. Although our judges are conscious of the fact that these arguments merge into each other and, more crucially, have not placed decisive reliance on any of them in isolation but looked at their cumulative effect, we shall here consider them separately. The arguments are basically four: (i) imposing liability on the public bodies in question would make bad economic sense; (ii) liability would inhibit the freedom of action of these bodies; (iii) it would be inappropriate for the courts to control elected bodies and tell them how to exercise their discretionary powers; and (iv) the victims in these cases had alternative remedies which make a tort remedy not only dangerous but also superfluous. We must examine these arguments in turn.

(i) Imposing liability on the public bodies in question would make bad economic sense

We call this set of reasons the "economic arguments" and note that in the English literature, it appears in a number of forms.

In the first, economic reasoning is invoked to explain why, in general, liability is not imposed in cases of pure omissions. As Lord Hoffmann put it in his judgment in *Stovin* v. *Wise*, the imposition of a duty of affirmative action upon a public body may result in its being required to confer an "externality", or unbargained-for benefit, upon a third party, in circumstances where this would lead to allocative inefficiency.[25] This rather technical economic explanation is examined in more detail in the next chapter. It seems not to have played a major part in Lord Hoffmann's reasoning in *Stovin* since he accepted later in his judgment that the "externality argument", while it might be of general relevance to the question of liability for omissions, did not really apply to public bodies since not only did they have the resources to act for the protection of third parties, they were also under pre-existing public law duties to act in any event.

In the second form, the emphasis is on the fact that a liability rule would force the public body in question to divert resources from other, potentially more important projects, to investigating its own actions or protect itself against possible claims. In *Hill* this argument appeared as a variation of the *Rondel* v. *Worsley*[26] argument:

"The trial of such actions would very often involve the retrial of matters which had already been tried . . .While no doubt many such actions would fail, preparing for and taking part in the trial of such

[25] [1996] 3 WLR 388, 406.
[26] [1969] 1 AC 210. It is, of course, interesting to note that this case is also currently under review by the European Court of Human Rights.

an action would inevitably involve considerable work and time for a police force, and thus either reduce the manpower available to detect crime or increase expenditure on police services."[27]

In the House of Lords, Lord Keith was of the same opinion when he said:

"A great deal of police time, trouble and expense might be expected to have to be put into the preparation of the defence to the action . . . the result would be a significant diversion of police manpower and attention from the most important function, that of the suppression of crime."[28]

The argument, understandably, resurfaces in the *Elguzouli* case where Lord Justice Steyn (as he then was) felt that an imposition of a duty of care would:

"introduce a risk that prosecutors would act so as to protect themselves from claims of negligence. The CPS would have to spend valuable time and use scarce resources in order to prevent lawsuits . . ."[29]

The argument also appears in *Stovin*, where Lord Hoffmann took the view that the imposition of liability would divert resources from other needs such as education and social services.[30] A few lines further down he put the economic argument in a slightly different way when he allowed himself the luxury of speculating that "one of the consequences of *Anns* . . . and the spate of cases that followed was that local council inspectors tended to insist upon stronger foundations than were necessary".

A third argument relates to insurance, and is again to be found in the judgment of Lord Hoffmann in *Stovin* v. *Wise*. Essentially, this is an argument to the effect that the losses incurred in cases involving maladministration by public bodies can most often be dealt with through insurance carried either by

---

[27] [1987] 2 WLR 1126, 1140, per Glidewell LJ.
[28] [1988] 1 WLR 1049, 1056.
[29] [1995] 2 WLR 173, 183.
[30] [1996] 3 WLR 388, 419.

the victim of harm or by some other party. Hence, in the context of the *Stovin* case, Lord Hoffmann argued that:

> "denial of liability does not leave the road user unprotected. Drivers of vehicles must take the highway network as they find it . . . It is primarily the duty of drivers of vehicles to take due care. And if . . . they do not, there is compulsory insurance to provide compensation to the victims."[31]

(ii) Liability would inhibit the free action of these bodies (the "inhibition argument")

In *Hill*, Lord Justice Glidewell put this argument in the following way:

> "if the police were liable to be sued . . . actions in this field would not be uncommon. Investigative police work is a matter of judgment, often no doubt dictated by experience and instinct. The threat of a decision which, in the end, proved to be wrong and might result in an action for damages would be likely to have an inhibiting effect on the exercise of that judgment."[32]

In the House of Lords Lord Keith echoed the same view when he said:

> "In some instances the imposition of liability may lead to the exercise of a function being carried on in a detrimentally defensive frame of mind."[33]

In the *Bedfordshire* case we again see this argument resurfacing in Lord Browne-Wilkinson's judgment when he stated that:

> "if a liability were to be imposed, it might well be that local authorities would adopt a more cautious and defensive approach to their duties. For example, as the Cleveland Report makes clear, on occasions the speedy decision to remove the child is sometimes vital. If the authority is to be made liable in damages for a negligent decision to remove a child (such negligence lying in the failure first to inves-

[31] [1996] 3 WLR 388, 419.

[32] [1987] 2 WLR 1126, 1140.

[33] [1988] 2 WLR 1049, 1055. See also *Olotu* v. *Home Office* [1997] 1 WLR 328.

tigate the allegation) there would be a substantial temptation to post-pone making such a decision until further inquiries have been made in the hope of getting more concrete facts. Not only would the child in fact being abused be prejudiced by such a delay: the increased workload inherent in making such investigations would reduce the time available to deal with other cases and other children."[34]

(iii) It would be wrong for the courts to second-guess public bodies in the exercise of their discretion (the "second-guess argument")

This clearly overlaps with the first and second policy arguments discussed above; but in the judgments it also appears as an independent policy heading. It thus plays a significant part in rejecting any idea of court interference where the decision of the public body lies in what was once termed the policy area. As Lord Browne-Wilkinson put it in the *Bedfordshire* case[35] "a common law duty of care in relation to the taking of decisions involving policy cannot exist". But an intervention by the court might become possible if the allegation of carelessness relates not to the taking of a discretionary decision but in the practical manner in which that act has been performed. The dividing line, however, between policy and operation (or, as some nowadays prefer it, justiciability) is sometimes more easily stated in theory than applied in practice. In some groups of cases, e.g., the police cases, the courts do not seem to have explored this distinction with any degree of thoroughness choosing, instead, to rely more heavily on the "scarce resources" argument in order to deny the imposition of any duty of care and, thus, any civil liability.[36]

(iv) In all these cases, the victims had alternative means of redress, which makes the tort remedy superfluous (the "alternative relief argument")

This argument also made its first appearance in the *Hill* case where the availability of some monetary compensation to the plaintiff through the Criminal Injuries Compensation Scheme

[34] [1995] 3 WLR 152, 184–5.
[35] Ibid., 173.
[36] See, for examples, the cases cited below at chapter 8, n. 11.

was noted by both Lord Justice Fox[37] and Lord Justice Glidewell.[38] The very same alternative remedy was noted as being available to the children in the *Essex County Council* case by Lord Justice Steuart Smith;[39] and this may have been a significant reason why he, unlike the other two Lord Justices, refused to recognise a tort duty towards the children. But in other cases, the *Bedfordshire* and the *Elguzouli* cases in particular, the judges came up with a veritable barrage of alternative remedies which, in their view, influenced their answer as to whether it was "fair, just and reasonable" to create a tort duty and thus a damages remedy in those cases. In this section we shall simply list these alternative remedies and later we shall review their effectiveness.

(a) Even where a duty of care can permissibly be imposed, its ambit and scope are significantly influenced by the statutory regime. If this provides a special complaint procedure, this will militate against the availability of an additional damages remedy.

(b) The imposition of a common law duty of care may cut across a complex statutory regime, often interdisciplinary in nature and requiring the participation of many different professions. To make one group of experts or civil servants liable instead of another would be wrong; to make them all liable, would be unfair.

(c) The decisions taken under the statutory regime may be subject to judicial review.

(d) The tort of malicious prosecution may be available to the plaintiff/victim. Alternatively, an action for misfeasance in public office may exist.

(e) A claim under the Criminal Injuries Compensation Scheme may be available to the victim.

---

[37] [1987] 2 WLR 1126, 1137.

[38] Ibid., 1140.

[39] [1998] 3 WLR 534, 549.

2. The reasons given by the French law in reaching its (contrary) conclusions

(a) The attitude of French law towards the policy arguments used by English decisions

(i) The "economic argument"

One cannot find in either French case law or doctrine any visible trace of the "economic argument" used in English law in any of its three forms. The interesting question is to determine why this way of reasoning is so manifestly absent from French writings. The reasons are likely to be the following.

Over the years, the French system of public liability has become mainly compensatory in nature and is deeply focused on the plaintiff and the reparation of his or her damage.[40] As a result, the Conseil d'Etat has, in recent years, regularly enlarged the scope of public liability for the sole purpose of protecting citizens who happen to be harmed by administrative activities. One way of doing this has been, as already stated, by reducing the number of situations in which a condition of gross fault is a prerequisite of liability. The most remarkable example of that evolution took place in 1992 when the condition was removed in cases involving liability of public hospitals.[41]

In the light of the above it would thus appear right to claim that French administrative law is more inspired by the idea of "risk socialisation" under which the law tends to admit that when citizens suffer damage of a certain type and size it is the duty of the state to compensate them even if it is not possible to link them with something which could be called misadministration. This vision explains that, in the recent past, several pieces of regulatory legislation were put into place in order to grant people compensation – from the state budget – for damages

---

[40] See, for instance, Christophe Guettier, *La résponsabilité administrative* (1996), 139; Michel Paillet, *La responsabilité administrative* (1996), 6.

[41] Conseil d'Etat, Assemblée, 10 avril 1992, Epoux V., *Recueil des arrêts du Conseil d'Etat,* 171, concl. H. Legal.

having sometimes no relation – or at least without the need of demonstrating any relation – to any administrative action or omission. We could thus mention here as illustrations a 1990 Act for victims of terrorist acts as well as a 1991 Act concerning people affected by by transfusions of blood contaminated by the AIDS virus.

Once the above "philosophical stance" is noted – even if not accepted – one can see why French judges are unlikely even to consider the cost that a liability rule might entail for the public authorities whose liability is the subject of litigation. Somewhat more surprisingly, the idea that such resources might be better used in another "public" context equally does not seem to be considered. Thus, in the kind of consumerist vision of public liability which has become predominant in French law, compensating the damages suffered by citizens because of administrative activities can never be a wrong use of public money; on the contrary, it may even be seen as the best possible use of public money when it is viewed as serving the principle of equality by avoiding a result that means that people who have randomly been affected by administrative action remain without compensation.

As to the second form of the "economic argument", based upon the consideration of insurance, its absence seems to have the following explanation. In some cases, the damage suffered is not compensated by any insurance; in others, it would certainly not be considered as compatible with the principles described above if the insurers could not recover from the administration the money they had paid to citizens harmed by its activity.

(ii) The "inhibition argument"

The "inhibition argument" is not unknown in French theory of public liability but it certainly plays a secondary part. This is so because, apart from its fundamental compensatory function, public liability is also viewed as a way of disciplining the administration: in that role, it complements judicial review, by imposing payment of compensation, whereas the former provides the annulment of illegal decisions.

However, it is clear that consideration of a possible inhibition that liability could cause in administrative action has exercised a certain influence, and is still exercising some influence, in certain cases in which liability is subject to the requirement that a gross fault be committed. This is particularly clear in the field of police and local authority activities, illustrated by the cases we mentioned as comparable to *Hill* and *Stovin*. Thus it is precisely because French administrative judges still think that the admission of liability for a simple fault would make the police (or local authorities) too cautious – and, therefore, less efficient – that they have maintained gross fault as a condition of liability – a precondition which, as already stated, has been abandoned in other areas of liability. The fluidity of the notion of "gross fault" and the consequences that may flow from it must, however, be repeated here.

(iii) The "second-guess argument"

Will a French administrative judge sometimes refrain from imposing public liability because he thinks that it would mean that he has second-guessed the public body in the exercise of its discretion? Such an approach would hardly strike a French judge as a natural one. The reason is the following. In practice, in a large majority of cases in which the administration is held liable, the fault, which has been identified, is an illegality. Illegality, in other words, is the most ordinary form of administrative fault.

This strong relation between fault and illegality has the consequence that the adjudication of administrative liability largely mirrors judicial review of administrative legality. The judges' attitude, when faced with questions of discretion, is the same in both cases. This means that judges have no reason to think that accepting liability would be especially impinging upon administrative discretion: they respect it, and review it to the same extent that they would otherwise do when reviewing questions of legality.

This does not mean that the "second-guess argument" plays

no role at all. It is obvious that some of the cases in which French administrative law has, as we have specified, accepted liability without fault, have been so treated because it allowed the judge to grant compensation without having to assess state behaviour, in fields where the public action is particularly difficult, and where it appears that decision-makers must be left with a large amount of discretion. It is partly in order to avoid a "second-guess" debate on the decision by which a person is detained in custody before trial that the 1970 Act mentioned above stated that state liability would arise without fault where a person detained is not ultimately sentenced. The "second guess" argument is thus turned on its head insofar as it seems to lead to an expansion, not a restriction of liability.

(iv) The "alternative relief argument"

It seems that in none of the cases we have mentioned, as comparable to the five paradigm English cases, could the consideration of an alternative relief coud have led the judges to exclude liability. In fact, there appears to be very few situations in which French administrative law could provide an adequate substitute to compensation granted on the ground of liability where damage has been suffered – the only example could be where somebody claims that he or she was refused by the administration a payment that he or she was entitled to receive, since that person can opt either for an action in liability or merely for the annulment of the refusal, with similar consequences if he or she succeeds.

Theoretically, there could be another alternative. In certain cases, the victim of damage caused by an administrative course of action can opt to act against civil servants instead of challenging the administration itself. This is so where the civil servants have committed what French law calls a personal fault – *faute personnelle* – and which corresponds to a very serious or intentional fault. In fact, however, this possibility will never be treated as "alternative relief" in the sense that its existence could lead the administrative judge to set aside administrative liability and direct the plaintiff towards private liability of a civil servant himself. Indeed, it has been ruled for a long time that, as far as the fault committed (be it a personal fault or not) has a link with the service, victims can act against the administration, which could then try to recover its money from a civil servant if he has committed a personal fault, and will not be driven towards the alternative of acting against the civil servant concerned.

(b) The actual reasons given by the French courts for the decisions

(i) Cases comparable to Hill

The way French decisions are worded shows clearly how free French administrative courts – compared to their English counterparts – are to act when they determine that an administrative fault has been committed. As mentioned above, French administrative courts operate within a very general and abstract concept of fault, which they apply with great flexibility. This appears from the fact that in two of the cases mentioned above, *Ville de Perpignan*,[42] and *Société Le Profil*,[43] the Conseil d'Etat not only did not feel obliged to characterise the duty which the administration might have neglected, it did not even state which statutory or regulatory rule had laid down the duty! In the third case, *M et Mme Garagnon*,[44] the infringed duty was identified more precisely. It was to be found in the rules that determine the special surveillance airport police must exercise when minors are taken abroad. However, the statutory or regulatory rules defining that duty were not specified by the Conseil d'Etat.

Another interesting aspect of these cases is the way they consider whether or not there has been a gross fault. Administrative courts usually solve that problem by using three kinds of criteria.[45] These are: the importance of the duty which was not properly fulfilled; the obviousness of the fault, illustrated by its

---

[42] Conseil d' Etat, 29 juillet 1948, *Recueil des arrêts du Conseil d' Etat*, 213.

[43] Conseil d' Etat, 26 avril 1979, *Recueil des arrêts du Conseil d' Etat*, 171.

[44] Conseil d' Etat, 26 juin 1985, *Recueil des arrêts du Conseil d' Etat*, 254.

[45] Michel Paillet, *La responsabilité administrative*, 122.

repetitiveness; and the size of the damage, which is sometimes a sign of how serious the fault is.

In none of the three cases is the criterion used made explicit. The case in which the reason why a gross fault was identified is most evident in *M et Mme Garagnon* – clearly, it was the importance of the duty to ensure that children are not taken abroad illegally.

(ii) Cases comparable to X v. Bedfordshire

In *M et Mme Pillon*[46] the exact nature of the duty which should have made the social service more careful in the placement of children, was not specified. On the contrary, in *Epoux Ouaras*[47] the Conseil d'Etat refered to certain provisions which, in the Public Health Code (*Code de la Santé Publique*) require that social services supervise the health of all children under a certain age.

(iii) Cases comparable to Stovin

Three aspects of *Commune de Maisons-Laffitte* and *Marabout*[48] are worth mentioning. The first is that only in *Commune de Maisons-Laffitte* do we find an indication of the statute from which the administrative duty derived. The reference, however, is actually very wide as it is more a reference to the general powers local authorities have over traffic and car parking, than to a particular provision which would define a precise obligation.

The second aspect is that in *Marabout* the Conseil d'Etat expressed the view that the local authority should have acted in order to free the street from illegal car parking "by a regulatory decision, or by direct action" (*prendre des mesures appropriées, réglementaires ou d'exécution*). Indeed, unlike English law, French administrative law on liability does not draw the distinction

[46] Conseil d' Etat, 4 mai 1983, No. 22811.

[47] Conseil d' Etat, 23 septembre 1987, *Recueil des arrêts du Conseil d' Etat*, 290.

[48] Conseil d' Etat, Assemblée, 200F 1972, *Ville de Paris c. Marabout, Actualité Juridique, Droit Asministratif*, novembre 1972, 597.

between policy and operation. Liability can arise either from wrong policy decisions – or the absence of them – as well as for wrong operational decisions – or the lack of them.

The third aspect is that, as the reader will already have realised, French administrative law on liability does not make a distinction between acts and omissions. Omission (*carence*) is a frequent cause of liability and there are no signs in case law that it would, in any intellectual sense, be treated in a different way than negligent acts.

(v) Cases comparable to Essex County.

For comparative purposes two points should be made about the case of *Consorts Fraticola*.[49] Once again, in that case, neither the legal source of the neglected duty, nor its precise content, are made explicit. We are given to understand that social services are under an obligation to look after children placed in foster families, and that these families are also obliged, on behalf of social services, to look after the children. But this is nowhere made clear in the judgment; and no statutory basis is mentioned.

The case also shows how the presumption of fault works in practice. As the *conclusions du commissaire du gouvernement*[50] show, the plaintiffs were not able to demonstrate that either social services, or the foster family had not been careful enough in looking after the child. The *commissaire du gouvernement* – and apparently the court after him – were satisfied that it was not fair to leave the burden of proof on the plaintiffs; instead, this burden had to be shifted to social services.

---

[49] C. adm. Bordeaux, 2 février 1998, *Consorts Fraticola, Les Petits Affiches*, 12 août 98, 3, concl. D Peane.

[50] Opinion given by a member of the court, who will not adjudicate in the sense that he or she will not vote when the decision is taken. In spite of the way this person is called, he or she does not represent the Government in any capacity.

3. German law

(a) The German attitude towards the kind of policy reasons advanced by English courts in order to reject these claims

All of the arguments advanced in English decisions against the imposition of liability have also been considered by the German legislator, courts and academics and, generally speaking, found wanting. For instance, the four policy considerations discussed above had been already considered at the time when BGB, § 839 was being enacted one hundred years ago. It would be wrong to think, as some scholars often do, that such policy-orientated discussions represent a novel form of reasoning found only in the common law. If there is any novelty in the use of such arguments it lies mainly in the fact that they appear prominently in the judicial decisions, themselves, rather than that they have been identified as useful, additional tools in the reaching of the final decision. More important, however, is the observation that these policy concerns, which hold such sway in the minds of one or two of the highest English judges, have been steadily loosing their appeal in contemporary German literature and judicial practice. The similarity with France is thus obvious, although the depth of the discussion that has taken place in Germany seems to be substantial.

The first two arguments – the "economic and inhibition arguments" – proved extremely controversial at the end of the last century.[51] It was thus stressed (as it is nowadays in England) that potential liabiltiy might make civil servants act too cautiously or expeditiously. But it was felt that even if this were to happen, and there were doubts whether in practice this would be the case, it would be better than any careless or less diligent behaviour on the part of the civil servants.[52] The same arguments also carried much weight with regard to the *personal*

[51] Mugdan, *Materialien zum BGB*, Vol. II, 1305; *Protokolle*, Vol. I, 609, 611; "liability would cause an unforeseeable heavy burden on the state". *Motive zu dem Entwurf des BGB*, Vol. II, 824.

[52] *Protokolle*, Vol. II, 662.

liability of the civil servant being sued. Thus, because of these considerations, it was *originally* argued that the civil servant should be liable *only* if he had acted maliciously or if his act amounted to a criminal offence.[53] In the event, however, the legislator decided not to adopt such a severe limitation of liability but, instead, chose to restrict the *personal* liability of the civil servant to solely negligent (but not intentional) acts whenever the injured person could obtain redress from another source (see discussion above). This limited restriction on liability was enacted in 1900 to secure that a person acting in an official function would not be inhibited by the fear of liability.[54] This argument carries little weight, however, if the public body is, itself, liable, an issue which had already been stressed in the consultations of the Committee which drafted the Civil Code. Liability of the state itself was thought to avoid the inhibition argument; but it was felt that this was not a matter for the Commission since the matter pertained to public law.[55] Besides this question the financial burden on the state had also been of great concern, especially with regard to certain categories of civil servants.[56] There was always the feeling, however, that it would be grossly unfair to leave a person affected by misconduct without recourse.[57] In addition, it must be stressed that the restriction does not play an important role in the present law, especially because courts have created many exceptions to the rule.[58] Only in a small percentage of cases can the state liability be reduced, and in those cases the amount of money involved is negligible.[59] There is, therefore, unanimous acceptance of the view that this

[53] Compare Staudinger and Engelmann, *BGB* (1st ed., 1901), § 839, n. 2; *Motive*, above at n. 51, Vol. II, 822. For a critical view of this restriction on the liability of the state, see Bettermann, "Vom Sinn der Amtshaftung" (1961) *JZ*, 482, 483; HJ Vogel, "Die Verwirklichung der Rechtsstaatsidee im Staatshaftungsrecht" *DVBl*, 1978, 657, 659.

[54] Vogel, ibid.

[55] *Protokolle*, Vol.II, 662.

[56] Jakobs and Schubert, *Beratungen des BGB, §§ 652–853* (1983), 1024.

[57] *Motive zu dem Entwurf des BGB*, Vol. II, 736 *et seq.*

[58] See Münchener, *Kommentar/Papier*, n. 296 and below.

[59] Compare *Zur Reform des Staatshaftungsrechts* (1976), 12, 69.

restriction should be abolished when the law is reformed (in accordance with what was said earlier in the book).

The danger that valuable time and resources might be spent in contesting the liability of public bodies has been raised as an argument against a general form of liability, i.e., a liability of the state even when all diligence had been observed (*generelle verschuldensunabhängige Haftung*). The argument has not been used, however, in the context of state liability where there has been a public wrong caused by a negligent act, where the protection of the individual is an issue, or where constitutionally guaranteed basic rights (such as life, health, liberty) are at stake.[60] In the latter cases in particular the argument is neutralised by the strong belief that an individual should be compensated for harm caused by a public body. This belief is regarded as an indispensable principle of the modern democratic state, and is taken very seriously.[61] Nor, finally, is this attitude affected by the distinction between "bad acts" and "omissions" which, again, seem to have weighed heavily in the minds of some senior English judges. *Hill* and *Elguzouli*, as well as their respective German parallels, thus show that harm can be caused by the public authority either when it fails to take the necessary decision to arrest a criminal promptly or where laxness results in an innocent person being kept in detention. The same would be true of the two child neglect cases in *Bedfordshire*: in the first case the authority wrongly declined to act, and in the second it acted wrongly.

The above-mentioned argument (the "inhibition argument") was relied upon by the district court (*Landgericht*) in the *criminal* prosecution of a social worker in the German equivalent of *Bedfordshire*.[62] The Court of Appeal reversed the decision of the *Landgericht* (which held the worker to be immune) because social workers are expected to decide, and in fact do decide, how

---

[60] Vogel, above at n. 53, 657, 662.

[61] *Zur Reform des Staatshaftungsrechts, Gemeinsame Arbeitsgruppe des Bundes und der Länder zur Neuregelung der Staatshaftung* (1987), 10; Ossenbühl, *Staatshaftungsrecht* (5th ed. 1998), 6.

[62] LG Osnabrück of 6 March 1996 in Mörsberger and Restemeier, *Helfen mit Risiko*, 121; see also 7.

to act according to their professional knowledge and experience and not because of fear of possible criminal sanctions.[63] Whatever one may think about this policy in criminal law, the situation with regard to the liability of the *state* for a public wrong is completely different.[64] Thus, on this matter German law lies closer to the view expressed by Lord Reid in the *Dorset Yacht* case[65] and has thus refused to adopt the argument that the imposition of liability could tempt civil servants to postpone vital decisions.

The argument that a liability rule might entail enormous financial consequences for the state has fared no better. A thorough empirical study, undertaken in connection with the reform proposals alluded to above, revealed that the financial burden of state liability (including all causes of action and not only breach of official duty) amounted to only to 0.015% of the total budget.[66] This may, in part, be due to the relative modest amount of damages which are awarded by German courts,[67] and to which we shall return below when we draw our comparative conclusions. At this stage, however, we will suppress the temptation of many English lawyers to dismiss the relevance of German law because of this difference in the level of awards. We must thus stress that, although the level of money compensation – especially for non-pecuniary damages – is not likely to be high,

[63] OLG Oldenburg of 2 September 1997, ZfJ 1997, 57; see also Oehlmann and Austermann op. cit.

[64] For the problems with regard to the duty to give warnings according to the new law on product security, see Tremml and Nolte, "Amtshaftung wegen behördlicher Warnungen nach dem Produktsicherheitsgesetz" *NJW* 1997, 2265.

[65] [1970] 2 WLR 1140, 1151: "It may be that public servants of the State of New York are so apprehensive, easily dissuaded from doing their duty and intent on preserving public funds from costly claims that they could be influenced in this way. But my experience leads me to believe that Her Majesty's servants are made of sterner stuff."

[66] *Zur Reform des Staatshaftungsrechts* (1976), 5, 71.

[67] For example the sum of DM 5.000, was awarded in 1988 for unlawful detention in a psychiatric institution for seven days. This amount, however, was only meant to provide compensation for non-pecuniary damages and did not include compensation for possible economic losses. OLG Oldenburg, *VersR*, 1991, 306. We return to this point in ch. 4.

61

affected plaintiffs do at least receive some satisfaction from the imposition of tort liability. More importantly, they can claim and do, in fact, receive, substantial compensation for economic losses which flow from the administrative action. Thus, readers will recall that in the German equivalent to the *Essex*[68] case the adopted parents received full economic losses, namely the cost of rearing and caring for the handicapped child (for life) whom they had been misled into adopting.

By contrast, the third policy argument – the "second guess argument" – for a time played an important role in German decisions. The Reichsgericht constantly held that the courts should not interfere with discretionary decisions of public bodies.[69] The courts could only decide in cases where the public body acted outside the ambit of its discretionary power.[70] Thus, only arbitrary actions and decisions which show an obvious error on the record can give rise to liability in tort. Like the policy/operational test, the non-use of discretion could also give rise to liability. Thus, in an early case comparable to *Elguzouli* the court held that the state prosecutor had a duty (not a discretionary power) either to end the proceedings or to institute proceedings before a court.[71] Yet the extremely restricted control has increasingly been considered to be excessive and, in addition, outdated with regard to notions of justice in a modern democratic state, in which public bodies, even when they have discretionary powers, are bound by the law. This means that they must make use of their discretion according to the purpose of the respective rule.[72] If a statutory rule thought to protect the interests of individuals also gives discretion to a public body,

[68] OLG Hamm, *FamRZ* 1993, 704.

[69] For reasons of simplicity we shall make no distinction between the two categories of discretionary power in German law, namely "Ermessen" and "Beurteilungsspielraum", which have slightly different demarcations and are subject to different ambits of judicial control.

[70] RG of 15 December 1939, RGZ 162, 273; RG of 8 November 1938, JW 1939, 239, 240; see also BGH of 17 January 1952, BGHZ 4, 302, 313 = NJW 1952, 583, 584.

[71] BGH of 8 March 1956, BGHZ 20, 178, 182.

[72] BGH of 15 February 1979, BGHZ 74, 144, 156 = NJW 1979, 1354, 1356.

justice requires that negligent use of the discretionary power causing harm to an individual should give rise to liability. Therefore, the restriction has been relaxed considerably – first with regard to judicial review of administrative acts by administrative courts,[73] and, subsequently, in public wrong cases raising issues of civil liability.[74] A discretionary decision may thus be reviewed by a court in a public wrong case even if it is within the ambit of discretion.[75] However, the court will not go into the question whether the decision taken by public body was "right" (*Richtigkeitsprüfung*) but only whether the decision seems plausible (*vertretbar*).[76] The test of plausibility allows far more control than was sanctioned in the past, but it still does not mean that the court is substituting its own judgment for that of the administrative authority. Thus, in a case that provides a close analogue to *Elguzouli* the court scrutinised the decision of the state prosecutor even though a court had approved the prosecutor's application for the warrant. This attitude must again be viewed in connection with the principle that public bodies are bound by the law (Article 20 II of the Constitution), that they must respect the law diligently,[77] and that these principles might not be surrendered for the sake of mere administrative convenience. The difference with English law is, thus, once again notable. More interestingly, however, experience shows that the

---

[73] Here one started with distinguishing between discretion and non-appliance of discretionary powers, misuse of discretion and reduction of discretion to only one possible decision.

[74] BGH of 15 February 1979, BGHZ 74, 144, 156 = NJW 1979, 1354, 1356; BGHZ of 12 July 1979, BGHZ 75, 120, 124 = NJW 1979, 1879.

[75] The discretion concerned in the following examples should be translated accurately as "*Beurteilungsspielraum*", not "*Ermessen*". Even if the errors involved do not give cause for appeal of an administrative decision (compare VwVfG, § 46 (*Verwaltungsverfahrensgesetz*) (Law of Administrative Procedure) the discretionary decision may give rise to a tort claim because it might not be unlikely that without the errors the discretionary decision would have been different; Münchener Kommentar/*Papier*, § 839, n. 203.

[76] BGH of 27 September 1990 – BGHR-BGB, § 839 Abs. 1 S. 1 Staatsanwalt 3; see also BGH of 21 April 1988, ZIP 1988, 921.

[77] Ossenbühl, *Staatshaftungsrecht* (5th ed 1996), 42.

liberalisation of judicial review has not entailed serious (let alone catastrophic) consequences in any economic or practical sense (e.g., an increase in volume of litigation). What common lawyers would thus describe as the "floodgates argument" has, in practice, proved to be an imagined (or invented) fear, but not a real problem.

Let us now move to the "alternative relief argument". Although the sum of money involved in state liability cases can, as already stated, be relatively small,[78] it is, in most cases, the only redress that the affected individual may have. In Germany, as in England, special compensation systems may in certain instances give some relief, as, for example, the Criminal Injuries Compensation Scheme in England or the payments under the German Law on Compensation for Criminal Prosecution.[79] Between those systems on one hand, and tort liability on the other, there is however, a notable difference, namely that in the latter case the injury was due to a careless act of the public body. In matters of justice the individual who has suffered a wrong can expect to be treated in a different way than someone who suffered misfortune.[80] In addition, the restriction on state liability in BGB, § 839 I 2 has, as already mentioned, little practical significance; it was relevant only with regard to 5.06% of all damages claimed.[81] The Federal Court of Justice thus described this rule as out of date, because the state should not conceal its liability behind possible payments made by others, such as private

[78] At least insofar as non-pecuniary damages are concerned. But see our observations in ch. 4.

[79] Which grants compensation for economic loss and – as far as detention is concerned – moral damages not exceeding DM 20,- per day: StrEG, § 7.

[80] In German law the claims under the Law on Compensation for Criminal Prosecution are independent of a faulty act of the public bodies concerned and may exist parallel to the tort claims as well as to claims under Article 5V of the European Convention on Human Rights, which concerns an unlawful (but not necessarily culpable) detention (BGH of 31 January 1966, BGHZ 45, 58; BGH of 29 April 1993, BGHZ 122, 268 = NJW 1993, 2927); Meyer, *Strafrechtsentschädigung und Auslagenerstattung* (4th ed. 1997), 36; BGH of 29 April 1993, VersR 1993, 792 = MDR 1993, 740.

[81] *Zur Reform des Staatshaftungsrechts* (1976) , 12, 95.

individuals.[82] Thus, exceptions to the exception regarding liability have been developed, namely with regard to certain kinds of redress and wrongs. If, for example, an employee of a public body travels with other road users, the alternative redress argument cannot be raised, because the public body is in the same-position as other users.[83] The same can be said with regard to the duty of public authorities to take care in their daily activities (*Verkehrssicherungspflicht*).[84]

More interesting for our purpose are the kinds of redress held irrelevant to state liability. Payments under the social security system as well as those under private insurance taken out by an injured individual (or somebody else other than the tortfeasor) are not regarded as "alternative redress". In the first case this is because social security should be able to recover damages paid by the tortfeasor so that the community of insured persons does not bear the costs of a public wrong.[85] With regard to private insurance it is considered that the injured person (or somebody else) has paid for that benefit and this should not be to the advantage of the tortfeasor.[86] More significantly, redress against other *public bodies* (in the form of alternative administrative remedies) is also held to be irrelevant for the purpose of BGB, § 839 I 2. This follows the principle accepted by German law

---

[82] BGH of 16 April 1964, BGHZ 42, 176 = NJW 1964, 1895; however, the court felt bound by the words of the statutes; only later groups of exceptions have been established (see below).

[83] BGH of 27 January 1977, BGHZ 68, 217, 220 = NJW 1977, 1238.

[84] The Federal Court of Justice applies the exception to the exception here: BGH of 10 July 1980, NJW 1980, 2194 (parallel case to *Stovin)*; BGH of 1 July 1993, BGHZ 123, 102, 104 = NJW 1993, 2613, 2616 (stability of trees – parallel case to *Ancell* v. *McDermott* [1993] 4 All ER 355; for critical remarks on this exception, see Münchener Kommentar/*Papier*, § 839, n. 310.

[85] BGH of 20 November 1980, BGHZ 79, 26 = NJW 1981, 623; BGH of 17 March 1983, NJW 1983, 2191; for the exclusion of continued payment of salary by the employer or the social security system, see also BGH of 20 June 1974, NJW 1974, 1767, 1860.

[86] BGH of 17 March 1983, NJW 1983, 2191; BGH of 28 October 1982, BGHZ 85, 230, 233 = NJW 1983, 1868; BGH of 2 April 1987, NJW 1987, 2664.

that public bodies are considered a unity.[87] Thus, we may summarise that in German law the alternative redress argument is regarded neither as an efficient nor a just restriction on state liability.

(b) Reasons given by the German courts reaching their conclusions

In the comparable case to *Hill* the main issue was whether the police owed an official duty towards the individual. With regard to the Public Prosecutor's Office such duty is owed towards the accused (and other persons involved in the investigation). Otherwise, however, German law has, in a long line of decisions, accepted that the duty of care is owed only to the State. The reason given was that the Office has duties only towards the community at large.[88] However, the same has not been held to be true of the police, which have repeatedly been held to owe a duty towards individuals. Thus, the police have been held to be under a duty to prevent the commission of criminal acts;[89] to trace stolen goods;[90] and to avoid the commission of torts.[91] It is said that this differentiation between police and public prosecution services is due to the different structure of their respective duties. The police are thus seen as the guardians of good order, and this is taken to mean that they must protect individual citizens as well. On the other hand, the Public Prosecutor is there to enforce the

[87] BGH of 12 April 1954, BGHZ 13, 88, 100.

[88] RG of 16 October 1923, RGZ 108, 249; RG of 24 March 1937, RGZ 154, 268; BGH of 28 March 1996, NJW 1996, 237, affirming OLG Düsseldorf of 7 August 1995, NJW 1996, 530 affirming LG Düsseldorf of 2 January 1995, ZIP 1995, 282; the state prosecutor, however, may have a duty of care towards a third party, if this individual has been involved in the investigation process: LG Trier of 13 January 1994, VersR 1994, 810. See, also, BGH of 16 October 1997, NJW 1998, 751.

[89] RG of 26 February 1935, RGZ 147, 144; see also LG Landshut of 14 September 1993, RuS 1994, 454.

[90] OGH Br.Z. Köln of 22 September 1950, NJW 1951, 112 – contrary to *Alexandreou* v. *Oxford* [1993] 4 All ER 328.

[91] BGH of 29 June 1989, BGHR BGB vor § 1/*Beweislast Amtshaftung* 1.

criminal law (*staatlicher Strafanspruch*[92]); and such a duty can be owed only towards the state. Although in the case discussed here the result seemed very clear because the police officers had acted with gross negligence,[93] the result did not depend on the fact that the police acted intentionally. In recent decisions concerning the Public Prosecutor the Federal Court of Justice has stated expressly that an action against the police would not fail in a comparable situation, because the police owed such duty to the individual.[94]

The existence of such duty had also been the central point of discussion in the parallel cases to *Stovin*[95] and *Essex*,[96] although the question arose whether there was any duty at all. Unlike *Stovin,* the distinction between omission and bad act did not play any role in the German decision. If there is a duty to make traffic safe, this duty can equally be breached through bad acts or omissions. Neither did the court consider that the public authority had any discretionary power; the authority could make only one decision, namely to ensure that visibility at the road intersection was not obstructed.

If the source of any danger is identified – which it was both in the English and German cases – it is the duty of the responsible authority to act in a timely manner.[97] The question whether the authority has acted in a timely manner, or whether there has been unnecessary delay, does not relate to the duty per se, but rather to the question of whether there has been any breach of this duty. Where it is impossible for the public authority to remedy all dangerous situations in a timely manner, such action would fail. The reason for its failure to impose liability would be lack of fault, and not reasons relating to discretion,

---

[92] Steffen, "Haftung für Amtspflichtverletzung des Staatsanwalts" (1972) *DriZ* 152.

[93] They had been lying before the court in order to protect the robbers.

[94] BGH of 28 March 1996, NJW 1996, 2376.

[95] BGH of 10 July 1980, NJW 1980, 2194.

[96] OLG Hamm of 15 July 1992, FamRZ 1993, 704.

[97] This is contrary to *Ancell* v. *McDermott* [1993] 4 All ER 355.

policy, or administrative expediency.[98] It is very likely that in German law the decision would remain the same even if the obstruction of visibility were caused by an object on an adjoining land, as was the case in *Stovin*.[99] Because of the importance of safety in traffic, the court had no doubt that the general duty for the safety of the roads (for every user) included the duty to ensure visibility at that intersection.

In the *Essex* parallel case the court argued that the duty of proper information, although not expressly provided for in a statute, resulted from the nature of the dealings and was laid down at least by the directives of the board. There was a fundamental duty towards the parents, and its breach caused considerable damage.[100] The contrast with the English case could thus now be more pronounced.

The problem that the exercise of discretion restricts judicial review was discussed, to some extent at least, in the parallel case to *Elguzouli*. For the reasons given above it did not, however, stop the court from imposing liability. As the discretionary decision taken by the public prosecutor – at that state of the investigations – was not plausible but, on the contrary, rendered carelessly, the court held that it was a negligent act justifying the liability of the state. A similar result was achieved in a case where

[98] See LG Berlin of 18 August 1994, VersR 1996, 603; LG Berlin of 24 June 1993, VRS 88, 1995, 7; OLG Sachsen Anhalt of 28.6.1996, VerkMitt 1996 No. 124 – all concerning bad road conditions in former East Germany; see also OLG Düsseldorf of 23 October 1997, NVwZ-RR 1998, 708, which concerned icy roads.

[99] Compare BGH of 28 May 1962, BGHZ 37, 165, 168, which held that a public authority is liable for dangers resulting from special street designs which adjoin rivers, ditches and so on; compare also with regard to tree branches above the road that might damage high lorries: OLG Sachsen Anhalt of 5 February 1997, DAR 1998, 18. However, it must be mentioned that a hedge obstructing the view in the twin case to *Stovin* (as well as the dangerous memorial in BGH of 28 May 1962, BGHZ 37, 165) was owned by the state.

[100] The Court of Appeal of Frankfurt argued in the same way in a recent case, but denied damages because of lack of fault: OLG Frankfurt of 22 January 1998, OLG-Rp Frankfurt 1998, 243. See also BGH of 2 April 1987, FamRZ 1987, 904 – the official guardian (*Amtspfleger*) had not warned the employer of the ward that the employee was likely to be a pyromaniac.

a person was kept in a psychiatric asylum as a result of an expert opinion concerning the state of his mind.[101] As well as detention, the discontinuation of criminal proceedings might also render a public authority liable if the decision is not "plausible".[102] In other instances, however, the courts have taken the view that the decisions were "plausible" and thus denied liability on the grounds that there was no fault.[103] Thus, from the point of view of German law, the important issue is that the Public Prosecutor has a duty of care towards the person charged with an offence and must thus therefore pay due respect and consideration to the legitimate interests of the person charged.[104]

In the case cited as parallel to *Bedfordshire* the topic of discretion was not raised because the statute was clear on this point: there was a duty to act in a certain way[105] and that duty was performed diligently.[106] If there had been any negligent act (or omission) on the part of the youth authority, liability in damages would have arisen (although it is an open question whether *moral* damages would be granted in such a (*tort*) action).[107]

[101] OLG Oldenburg of 20 May 1988, VersR 1991, 306.

[102] BGH of 21 April 1988, NJW 1989, 96, 98.

[103] BGH of 22 February 1989, BGH-DAT Zivil; BGH of 27 September 1990, BGHR BGB, § 839 Abs. 1 S. 1 Staatsanwalt 3.

[104] For example especially with regard to the information given to the public: OLG Hamm of 15 July 1992, NJW 1993, 2109. This applies also to the police: BGH of 16 January 1961, BGHZ 34, 184; BGH of 19 January 1989, 1989, 1024; OLG Hamburg of 2 November 1978, NJW 1980, 842. Of course, this role of the state prosecutor in German law differs from the English adversary system considerably. In German criminal procedure there is no adversary proceeding and the prosecutor is obliged also to reveal facts and circumstances which are in favour of the accused (StPO, § 160II) (see also BGH of 8 March 1956, BGHZ 20, 178, 180), but this was not the vital point in the decisions cited above.

[105] Lakies, "Vorläufige Maßnahmen zum Schutze von Kindern und Jugendlichen nach §§ 42, 43 Kinder- und Jugendhilfegesetz (KJHG)" (1992) *ZfJ* 49, at 51.

[106] Were the facts exactly as in *Newham* there would arise the question in German law of whether the expert himself would be liable; compare BVerfG of 11 October 1978, NJW 1979, 305.

[107] BGB, § 847 in combination with BGB, § 253 restrict moral damages to injuries of body, health and liberty; serious infringement on the right to person-

There are many cases, however, where the local youth authority caused economic loss to the child through negligent acts, and in these cases the state was held liable because the youth authority owed a duty of care towards the child.[108] The same is true with regard to negligent acts of a family court judge when authorising dealings of the guardian or the parent.[109] Had there been any tort case comparable to the first case in *Bedfordshire*, there is little doubt that a German court would have gone into the matter in detail and would have allowed evidence on the question of carelessness. That the criminal proceedings against the social worker (in the comparable German case) were finally stayed,[110] should not be taken as indicating that a tort action would fail; at the very least, it would have been tried and not, as

ality (*Persönlichkeitsrechtsverletzungen*) has been held to give rise to moral damages (BVerfG of 14 February 1973, BVerfGE 34, 269, NJW 1973, 1221; compare Markesinis, *The Law of Obligations, Vol. II, The Law of Torts*, 927), but here it would be questionable whether the same applies to parental rights (which are also protected in BGB, § 823I) and, if not, whether the negligent act also injured the right of personality of the mother.

[108] OLG Celle of 18 September 1996, NJW-RR 1997, 135, concerning advice with regard to maintenance; OLG Köln of 10 January 1991, FamRZ 1991, 1098 – the guardian gave days of grace for maintenance payments to the father; the Federal Court of Justice also awarded damages to the guardian, because the local youth authority had caused economic loss, BGH of 15 June 1989, DAVorm 1989, 864. There has been some controversy over whether a local youth authority or an official guardian (*Amtspfleger*) acts in the exercise of a public office (denied by OVG Münster of 6 March 1978, NJW 1979, 1220, 1221), but the overwhelming opinion especially in liability cases affirms this – see, for example, OLG Celle of 16 August 1996, NJW-RR 1997, 135, expressly affirming the official function of the official guardian: BGH of 5 May 1983, FamRZ 1983, 1220. There may also be liability of the state for the negligent act of the guardian towards third parties, for example the employer of a ward, who should have been warned by the guardian that the ward was a pyromaniac (this case is comparable to the *Essex* case): BGH of 2 April 1987, FamRZ 1987, 904.

[109] BGH of 31 March 1960, BGHZ 33, 136, 140 – no proper control of guardian; BGH of 20 November 1967, VersR 1968, 172 – no proper representation of child.

[110] After the OLG Oldenburg ZfJ 1997, 55 had allowed the appeal, the *Landgericht* stayed the proceedings because, if there had been any fault of the accused, it was only a minor fault (StPO, § 153).

in England, been struck out.[111] There is thus a duty of care on the local youth authority to protect neglected or misused children,[112] as soon as the authority obtains knowledge of the neglect or misuse.[113] It is another question, however, in what situation the conduct of the social worker will amount to a breach of that duty and it is a further and very delicate question of when it should be regarded as negligent.

[111] For the problems resulting especially from criminal proceedings against social workers, see Mörsberger/Restemeier, *Helfen mit Risiko* (1997).

[112] The law, however, does not give a right to claim performance of that duty (*öffentlich-rechtlicher Erfüllungsanspruch*): Gerauer, "Die Struktur der Jugendhilfe im neuen Kinder- und Jugendhilfegesetz (KJHG)" *DAVorm* 1990, 495, 497.

[113] Hauck, Haines and Mainberger, *Sozialgesetzbuch* (SGB VIII) 23 (loose-leaf-service 1998), K 42, n. 15, K 51, n. 23, K 53, n. 13, K 55, n. 55. The Court of Appeal of Oldenburg (ZfJ 1997, 55) even held that a social worker has the role of a guarantor towards a child (*Garantenstellung*), i.e., in criminal law a role which obliges the social worker to act when the life and well-being of a child is endangered.

3
A Critique of the English Reasons

1. How convincing are the English arguments?

Since the five English cases discussed in this book have reached, as we have seen, their conclusions predominantly by reference to a number of openly stated policy factors, the continued viability of their results will depend upon whether future generations of practitioners, with or without the assistance of academic writers, are able to challenge the validity of their arguments. Of course, practitioners acting for aggrieved plaintiffs may also try to avoid the restrictive results of these decisions by falling back on the time-honoured way of distinguishing their own case from an apparently binding and adverse older ruling. There are some signs that in the area of police powers this has already happened.[1] However, in this context one must also note that the chances of this being accepted is becoming increasingly difficult as *dicta* from various "striking out" cases are piling up in a direction that is consistently favouring defendants.[2] This accumulation of such pro-defendant authority thus makes it nearly impossible for impecunious but deserving plaintiffs even to contemplate asserting in a judicial context that their case justifies being treated as an exception to the immunity trend. Indeed, one of the authors of the *Hill*[3] judgment admitted as much in one of his subsequent judicial opinions.[4]

[1] Thus, *cf. Swinney* v. *Chief Constable of Northumbria Police Force* [1996] 3 WLR 968, with *Olotu* v. *Home Office* [1997] 1 WLR 328.

[2] We consider later the effect that *Barrett* v. *Enfield* – [1999] 3 WLR 79 – may have on this trend. Here, it is sufficient to state our belief that *Barrett* (in the House of Lords) would not have come about if it had not been for *Osman* and the kind of arguments we are advancing in this work.

[3] *Hill* v. *Chief Constable of West Yorkshire* [1988] 1 WLR 1049.

[4] *Alexandrou* v. *Oxford* [1993] 4 All ER 328, 340: "the observations . . . in

On the other hand, practitioners will also have to take increasing note of the fact that Strasbourg is showing signs of unease over such blanket immunities which it sees, not without cause, as capable of amounting to a denial of access to justice under Article 6 (1) of the European Convention of Human Rights. To the extent that this is correct, the European Court of Human Rights is prepared to voice some disapproval[5] – a disapproval which we venture to suggest will grow as our own Human Rights Act begins to exert a serious influence over the entire range of private law. Since, on the whole, we would welcome this development, we must now turn to examine the validity of the policy reasons advanced by our judges against tort liability in the hope to prove them unconvincing.

At first glance the policy arguments advanced by our courts seem overwhelming. The prestige of the judges who have advanced them – for instance Lord Browne-Wilkinson, Lord Steyn and Lord Hoffmann – coupled with the confident style in which these policy views have been presented to the legal public – seem to confer upon them an aura of inevitability. These very same features, however, can also lead lawyers to forget that in some of the leading cases the final outcome of the litigation was opposed by most of the judges who heard the case. Of course, in precedental terms, what matters is the final count in the House of Lords. Analytically, however, pointing out the fact that there already exists serious division in judicial opinion can only strengthen the conviction that if these policy reasons can be challenged head on, the outcome they have produced may not be as unshakeable as may appear at first sight. This

Hill's case in relation to the effect on the police of their being potentially liable in negligence were general, not limited to the facts of that case". Although this must now be read in the light of the observations in *Swinney* v. *Chief Constable of Northumbria Police Force* [1996] 3 WLR 968, the immunity granted to the police is, in practice, a blanket one; and this is how the Strasbourg court considered matters in its *Osman* judgment.

[5] We return to this issue below but note here that English lawyers are likely to see *Osman* as an impermissible example of judicial activism. Even if that is so, however, in our view they will have to learn to live with it.

argument is further strengthened by the realisation, supported by growing judicial and extra-judicial pronouncements, that the philosophical starting point of our judges is no longer as uniform as it may have been fifty or even thirty years ago.[6] Our point is thus really this: the doctrine of binding precedent may, for the time being, be giving the impression that our law has taken an irreversible turn towards defendants, but this does not imply that this change is here to stay. Our belief in the opposite conclusion lies in our conviction that the policy reasons given by our judges are, on closer examination, much less convincing than their proponents make them out to be.

We will divide our analysis into a number of sections. We will thus consider first the group of reasons that are based on economic arguments. Secondly, we will analyse a set of justifications, which could be thought of as being broadly constitutional in nature: these refer to the division of powers between the executive and the courts and to the possibility of obtaining alternative remedies. Thirdly, we will examine the question of how far the reasoning in these cases has led to inconsistency of treatment in the application of the law. We will conclude by looking at the relationship between tort law and human rights.

---

[6] That these philosophies may be radically different can be seen from the starting point adopted by two of our most learned judges. Thus, in the *Bedfordshire* case (*X (Minors)* v. *Bedfordshire County Council* [1994] 2 WLR 554, 572F) Sir Thomas Bingham MR (as he then was) said: 'If [the child] can make good her complaints . . ., it would require very potent considerations of public policy, which do not in my view exist here, to override the rule of public policy, *which has first claim on the loyalty of the law: that wrongs should be remedied*'. (emphasis added). In *Stovin* v. *Wise* [1996] 3 WLR 388, on the other hand, Lord Hoffmann seemed to adopt a different starting point when he said "the assumption from which one starts makes a great deal of difference . . . The trend of authorities has been to discourage the assumption that anyone who suffers loss is prima facie entitled to compensation from a person . . . whose act or omission can be said to have caused it. *The default position is that he is not*" (emphasis added). Most judges, however, would not take such a clear stand, even if in the end they leaned in Lord Hoffmann's direction. Thus, see Lord Browne Wilkinson's views in the *Bedfordshire* case [1995] 3 WLR 152, 183B).

(a) Economic reasoning

As we saw in Chapter Two, three broad types of economic arguments were offered. These relate, respectively, to externalities, defensive practices, and insurance. We will consider them in turn and then analyse a fourth reason not cited explicitly by the courts but referred to somewhat indirectly by Lord Hoffmann: this we call the "defendant of last resort" argument.

(i) Economics opposes the imposition of duties of affirmative action where this would lead to externalities in the form of unbargained-for benefits

This argument was very clearly expressed by Lord Hoffmann in the following passage in *Stovin* v. *Wise*:

> "In economic terms, the efficient allocation of resources usually requires that an activity should bear its own costs. If it benefits from being able to impose some of its costs on other people (what economists call 'externalities') the market is distorted because the activity appears cheaper than it really is. So liability to pay compensation for loss caused by negligent conduct acts as a deterrent against increasing the cost of the activity to the community and reduces externalities. But there is no similar justification for requiring a person who is not doing anything to spend money on behalf of someone else . . . So there must be some special reason why he has to put his hand in his pocket."[7]

As Lord Hoffmann indicates, a general rule imposing liability for omissions could well lead to inefficiency. Just as an activity which causes negative externalities without incurring liability for them receives, in effect, a subsidy from tort law, so activities which give rise to obligations of affirmative action in the absence of any reciprocal benefit are being penalised by the legal liability system. We would therefore expect there to be under-provision of the activities in question.

Important and helpful *in general* though this passage in Lord Hoffmann's speech may be, it does not particularly help his own argument against the imposition of liability upon public bodies.

[7] [1996] 3 WLR 388, 406.

Lord Hoffmann himself recognised that it has no application in situations of reliance or interdependence between plaintiff and defendant: "[t]here may be a duty to act if one has undertaken to do so or induced a person to rely upon one doing so". The exchange of reciprocal benefits or burdens between the parties may make it appropriate for an affirmative duty to be imposed, since the element of one-sided subsidy no longer exists. In fact, most of the situations in which English law imposes a duty of affirmative action are either like this (liability rarely arises between strangers) or involve the imposition of liability on the party who has the resources to deal with a particular threat of harm (such as an occupier or landowner).

In *Stovin* v. *Wise* the relationship between the parties was that of strangers;[8] at least we can say that there was no relevant, pre-existing relationship between the plaintiff and the council. Such was clearly not the case, however, in *W* v. *Essex County Council*[9] (which in any event is hard to see as an omission case). Not only were the parties known to each other prior to the harm occurring; the council had given an undertaking not to do the very thing, it then did. In *Osman* v. *Ferguson*[10] the parties were known to each other and there was, arguably, an element of reliance by the deceased on the police with regard to his own safety as well as that of his son.

There are other reasons for treating the act/omission distinction with scepticism in the context of cases such as *Stovin* v. *Wise*. We shall offer two.

First, public authorities do have the resources to act in such a way as to obviate dangers to third parties. Thus, they are not excluded from liability by virtue of the need, as stated by Lord Wilberforce in *Goldman* v. *Hargrave*,[11] to take into account the actual resources available to a defendant upon whom a duty of affirmative action might be imposed. As Lord Hoffmann himself said:

[8] The point is considered at length by Lord Hoffmann, ibid., 406 *ff*.
[9] [1998] 3 WLR 534.
[10] [1993] 4 All ER 344.
[11] [1967] 1 WLR 645.

"It is certainly true that some of the arguments against liability for omissions do not apply to public bodies like a highway authority. There is no 'why pick on me' argument: as Kennedy LJ said [in the Court of Appeal[12]], the highway authority alone had the financial and physical resources, as well as the legal powers, to eliminate the hazard."[13]

Secondly, in cases involving public authorities, the defendant is normally under some kind of pre-existing public law obligation to act. Where this is the case, we cannot speak of an affirmative obligation being created *de novo*. Nor would it be possible to argue that the imposition of liability would lead to the under-provision of the service or activity in question. This point was recognised by Lord Nicholls in *Stovin* v. *Wise* when he said:

"if there were a common law obligation in the present case, sounding in damages, the extent of the obligation would march hand in hand with the authority's public law obligations. This is a cardinal feature of the present case. The council's public law obligation was to act as a reasonable authority. The common law obligation would be to the same effect."[14]

(ii) Imposing liability on public authorities will lead to inefficiency in the form of 'defensive administration' and the diversion of expenditure

In his judgment in *Stovin* v. *Wise*,[15] Lord Hoffmann argued that:

"the creation of a duty of care upon a highway authority, even on grounds of irrationality in failing to exercise a power, would inevitably expose the authority's budgetary decisions to judicial inquiry. This would distort the priorities of local authorities, which would be bound to try to play safe by increasing their spending on road improvements rather than risk enormous liabilities for personal injury accidents. They will spend less on education or social services.

[12] [1994] 1 WLR 1124, 1139.
[13] [1996] 3 WLR 388, 408.
[14] Ibid., 398–9.
[15] Ibid., 419.

> I think that it is important, before extending the duty of care owed by public authorities, to consider the cost to the community of the defensive measures which they are likely to take in order to avoid liability."

As we saw above, similar arguments were made by Lord Brown Wilkinson in the *Bedfordshire* case, by Lord Justice Steyn in *Elgozouli-Daf*,[16] and by Lord Keith in *Hill*.

The claim that negligence liability leads to "defensive practices" is often made in this and related contexts. However, the evidence on which it rests remains slim. Some US studies have found evidence that expenditure on bureaucratic and administrative procedures designed to avoid liability for medical negligence, such as various kinds of form-filling and checking, has grown considerably in recent years and now amount to billions of dollars across the system as a whole.[17] No similar studies have been carried out for the United Kingdom or the public service elsewhere.

Lord Hoffmann's suggestion that, after *Anns*, local inspectors insisted on "stronger foundations than was necessary" is therefore just speculation. We could answer Lord Hoffmann's hunch with a counter hunch, namely, that while it is possible that the post-*Anns* regime led to unnecessarily strong and expensive foundation, the post-*Murphy* situation may be encouraging sloppy verification of building calculations. What the law must, surely, be striving to achieve is neither excessive caution nor unnecessary sloppiness; and the latter may well follow a signal from the courts that they are opposed to any form of civil liability. Legal arguments cannot be solved, and litigation cannot be determined, on the basis of hunches, however eminent and experienced their source may be. Moreover, hunch or intuition, the dividing line between what is prudent and what becomes excessive is a fine one. At present, we do not have enough empirical evidence to guide us in the matter of foundation

---

[16] *Elgozouli-Daf* v. *Commissioner of Police of the Metropolis* [1995] 2 WLR 173.

[17] Dewees, Duff and Trebilcock, *Exploring the Domain of Accidents Law*, *op. cit.*, ch. 5, review this evidence.

inspections; and what we do have from another area of the law – medical malpractice – may suggest that one person's excessive caution is another's prudent practice. In another case,[18] Lord Hoffmann was prepared to be more candid and admit that the absence of empirical evidence makes it difficult to predict the economic consequences of a pro-liability decision; so why not show the same candour here and avoid alarmist statements? In short, we submit that an economic analysis of a decision requires more than our judges have so far been able to produce.

What is also problematic for this argument is that it could apply with equal force to well-established areas of tortious liability, such as employers' liability and product liability. The argument is not unique to the liability of public authorities. Indeed, from this point of view the case for granting immunity to public authorities (via the concept of duty of care) is weaker still, since they are not subject to the forces of competition, nor to the same damaging reputational effects of litigation which affect private sector organisations.

In other contexts, the courts have been sceptical of arguments about the inhibitive effect that civil liability would have on the actors. In *Dorset Yacht*, Lord Reid had no time for such arguments.[19] In *Spring*, the House of Lords unanimously rejected a variant of this argument, and the sky has not yet fallen on our heads. Yet another variant of this point appeared in *Rondel* v. *Worsley*[20] and there it won the day. The signs are that Strasbourg, again, may remind us that continental European advocates are also subject to duties towards their courts and judges along with their duties to their clients. Their potential liability for negligent conduct has not caused them to be less honest, less forthright, or less effective than our barristers; and compulsory insurance has ensured that they have not suffered financial ruination as a result of a liability rule. Our brief comparative survey suggests that the potential of civil liability has not made con-

[18] *White* v. *Chief Constable of South Yorkshire Police* [1998] 3 WLR 1510, 1556.
[19] [1970] 2 WLR 1140, 1151.
[20] [1969] 1 AC 191.

tinental police, local authorities or social security agencies less prompt, less efficient or less effective. The judges' arguments that apocalyptic consequences would follow if our system went the same way may thus sound attractive on paper but, in their extreme form, they are, once again, unsupported by any empirical evidence. The most recent pronouncement on this type of case – *Barrett* v. *Enflield London Borough Council*[21] – may provide some evidence that this point is getting through to some judges. Thus, in *Barrett* Lord Hutton opined that he "would not give this consideration great weight".[22] This statement was preceded, however, by the words, "In the circumstances of this case", and this could be seen as an important proviso given that Lord Hutton was keen to stress that the *Bedfordshire* arguments carried "insufficient weight" in the case which he was actually deciding. On the other hand, the learned Lord coupled his "dislike" of the "inhibition argument" with an express approval of a wider *dictum* by Lord Justice Evans in the Court of Appeal phase of the *Barrett*[23] hearing, and this could give a wider significance to Lord Hutton phrase.

(iii) First party insurance is a more effective way of spreading the loss than imposing liability upon public bodies

As we saw earlier, insurance arguments feature in Lord Hoffman's judgment in *Stovin* v. *Wise* as well as in some of the other cases under consideration here. The broader case for reducing the role of liability and, by extension, of liability or third party insurance, in favour of loss or first party insurance, has been made by Professor Patrick Atiyah. In *The Damages Lottery*, Atiyah argues that the liability system is both inefficient, because it gives rise to wasteful double insurance – first party and third party – and regressive, in the sense that higher prices

[21] [1999] 3 WLR 79.

[22] Ibid., 114.

[23] There, the Lord Justice had argued that "if the conduct in question is of a kind which can be measured against the standards of the reasonable man, placed as the defendant was, then I do not see why the law in the public interest should not recognise those standards to be observed" ([1998] QB 367, 380).

and inefficient public services hit the poor hardest. First party insurance, he claims, would be preferable because only those who considered it worthwhile to insure would pay the premiums to do so.[24]

It is often assumed that the existence of liability insurance creates waste within the third category of accident costs identified by Calabresi, those relating to the administration of the system, while doing little to promote efficient precautions in relation to the second category. However, there is some empirical evidence to suggest that the abolition of liability and its replacement by private loss insurance lead to an increase in accident rates. This can be seen from "before and after studies" that looked at jurisdictions which abolished liability in tort for road traffic accidents and replaced it with a system based on first party insurance. In Quebec, the rate of increase in accidents was, according to various accounts, between 10% and 30%.[25] Insurance can, it seems, have a deterrent effect if premiums and bonuses are related to the experience of individual policyholders. This is true even of first party insurance. If first party insurance is "experience rated" – in other words, the less experienced pay higher premiums – the system incorporates an incentive to improve the standard of care.

In general, it is not at all clear from the present state of research in this area that we should prefer a tort regime in which fault plays no role. The system of fault plus liability insurance will often be a more effective deterrent than a no-fault scheme. Liability insurance is important from an economic point of view because it attaches implicit prices to dangerous activities. In this way, "the direct incentives of the liability system may be trans-

[24] *The Damages Lottery*, (Hart, 1997) 134.

[25] Dewees, Duff and Trebikock, *Exploring the Domain of Accident Law*, *op. cit.* (OUP, 1996) 25, citing M Gaudry, "The effects on road safety of the compulsory insurance, flat premium rating and no-fault features of the 1978 Quebec Automobile Act", in Osborne Commission, *Report of Inquiry into Motor Vehicle Accident Compensation in Ontario* (Toronto: Queens' Printer); R Devlin, "Liability versus no-fault Automobile Insurance Regimes: An Analysis of the Experience in Quebec", PhD Thesis, University of Toronto.

lated into the terms of insurance policies".[26] Insurers have an incentive to monitor the activities of the insured and set premiums according to how far they act to reduce the risk of harms to third parties. While this implicit pricing will not work well if insurance societies operate on the basis of "knock for knock" – effectively allowing claims to cancel each other out – this practice is, it seems, fading away in Britain for the very reason that it involves the cross-subsidisation of dangerous activities by the less dangerous, and hence is not in the long-term interests of insurance companies.[27] Hence, it is not necessarily the case that defendants can simply pass on the costs of liability if they have third party insurance. It seems that both the level of activity and the degree of care taken by defendants can both be affected through the operation of liability when coupled with insurance.

This is demonstrated by the studies of North American workers' compensation schemes. In such schemes, it is the employers who have to take out insurance, not the employees. Insurance premiums end up being varied by industry and, more rarely, by firm. The most carefully constructed empirical studies – those which cater for the fact that the introduction of no-fault compensation leads to an increase in the number of injuries which get *reported* – found that increases in workers' compensation benefits led to a reduction in injury rates, and that the reduction was most substantial for high-risk industries and high-risk firms.[28] This evidence supports the claim that risk-related liability insurance helps reduce accident rates, in addition to providing for a degree of loss spreading.

[26] Shavell, "Economic Analysis of Law" (1999) *NBER Reporter* (Spring), 12, 13.

[27] This has been extensively reported in the insurance and financial press. See e.g. N Richardson, "Motor Insurance Myth Hits the Crash Barrier" *The Independent*, 23 March 1996. We are grateful to Mr David Howarth of Clare College, Cambridge, for this reference and for most helpful discussion on this point.

[28] M Moore and WK Viscusi, *Compensation Mechanisms for Job Risks: Wages, Workers' Compensation and Product Liability* (Princeton: Princeton University Press, 1990); Dewees, Duff and Trebilcock, *Exploring the Domain of Accident Law*, above at n. 25.

In short, to argue that liability insurance necessarily involves waste and inefficiency within the system of accident compensation as a whole is to fail to understand the complex economic effects to which this form of loss-spreading gives rise. The optimal or ideal form of insurance depends in practice on a range of factors which include the relative wealth of the parties concerned (how effectively can they meet claims in the absence of insurance?) and the ability of insurers to observe and verify the risk-reducing activities of the insured. In some circumstances, it may be economically efficient to impose a statutory obligation on certain parties to take out liability insurance, as is currently the case in many areas of accident law. This would be so, for example, if those taking part in risk-creating activities would not, in the absence of insurance, have the means to meet claims against them. In some cases, economists suggest that the legislator should intervene to make liability insurance unlawful – this would be efficient where insurers could not effectively monitor risk-reducing activities and vary premiums accordingly. The legislator also has an interest in regulating attempts by potential defendants to render themselves "judgment-proof" by various devices aimed at evading liability (we return to this point below in the context of our discussion of the "defendant of last resort" argument).

To resolve these questions is a complex matter. As Professor Steven Shavell has suggested:

> "[t]o understand when and how to regulate liability insurance, these points need to be explored, and data needs to be developed and analysed on the nature of the judgment-proof problem and of liability insurance coverage in various areas of risk."[29]

These are are issues which probably require the kind of systematic consideration of policy options which only the legislator can effectively engage in. What, then, is the message for the courts? The issue for them is not whether and how to regulate liability insurance, but whether to create a demand for this type

[29] "Economic Analysis of Law", above at n. 26, 14.

of insurance in the first place by imposing liability. As we have seen, the economic arguments for and against liability insurance are finely balanced; but they certainly do not point towards it being necessarily inefficient and wasteful. On the contrary, it may play a vital role in signalling to potential defendants the means by which they can reduce risks of harm to third parties.

This insight is just as relevant to the behaviour of statutory bodies and public authorities as it is to manufacturers, occupiers and employers. Where public bodies carry third party insurance, we would expect insurance companies to monitor their internal processes for assessing and managing risk, in this way contributing to improved effectiveness in the delivery of public services. Where, alternatively, public bodies operate on the basis of self-insurance – in other words, carrying sufficient funds to meet potential claims – they have just as strong an incentive to avoid incurring liability for negligence. As David Howarth has pointed out,[29a] negligent local authorities in this position will either have fewer resources to meet their policy objectives, or will have to raise taxes to make up the difference and explain to voters why they are doing so. If, therefore, the courts were to grant sweeping immunities to public bodies, they would in effect be negating one of the principal mechanisms by which overall costs within the accident compensation system – not just the costs of accidents themselves but also the costs of precautions and the costs of administering compensation – are minimised.

This is not to suggest that the practice of liability insurance is always efficient. However, the answer to inefficiency, in this context, lies not in the abolition of liability, but rather in the regulation of insurance practices, as we have just explained. The history of liability insurance suggests that the legislator is ready to intervene to make insurance compulsory where this is socially and economically desirable. There is no, good, economic reason for courts to short-circuit this process by denying liability on the part of whole classes of defendants through the use of the duty

[29a] D Howarth, review of P.S. Atiyah, The Damages Lottery, in *The Times Literary Supplement*, 5 June 1998.

concept. Indeed, from an economic viewpoint there is every reason for them not to take this step.

(iv) Public bodies need special protection as "defendants of last resort"

An argument which did not figure prominently in the judgments of the five cases we are considering here, but which has been discussed in the context of the academic debate and is implicit in some of Lord Hoffmann's comments in *Stovin* v. *Wise*, is the idea that public bodies are at risk of speculative litigation in a way which most individuals and private-sector companies are not. The idea is that public authorities are liable to become "defendants of last resort" since they are unable to escape liability in ways which are open to other types of defendants. The most obvious way in which other defendants do this is through bankruptcy or insolvency. Strategies for avoiding liability through the use of shell companies which protect the parent company from legal claims are well advanced in the United States, to the extent that commentators there have referred to the prospect of the "death of liability" if current trends continue.[30]

This practice does not appear so widespread in Britain, but we are certainly familiar with the idea that public authorities may end up as residual defendants when all else fails. Thus, it has been suggested that the difficulty which home owners have in tracking down and obtaining damages from negligent builders explains why, in the line of cases culminating in *Murphy* v. *Brentwood District Council*,[31] it was local authorities which bore the force of litigation in respect of defective premises. Even where a builder can be traced and has sufficient assets to be worth suing, contribution between joint tortfeasors means that the builder's negligence is, to some extent, underwritten by the resources of the local authority: the activities of negligent private sector defendants are then subsidised by the public purse.[32]

---

[30] See L LoPucki, "The Death of Liability" (1996) 106 *Yale Law Journal* 1.

[31] [1991] 1 AC 398.

[32] See T Weir, "Governmental Liability" [1989] *Public Law* 40.

In our view, this is the *only* "economic" argument which could justify treating public authorities as a special case through the device of the duty of care. All the other arguments considered here either fail to stand up to close economic scrutiny (such as the insurance argument), or, insofar as they survive such scrutiny, could be applied with equal force to cases involving private-sector defendants (such as the defensive administration argument).

However, in accepting that the danger of speculative litigation against public bodies is a real one, we do not need to accept a near-blanket denial of liability of the kind which the law appears to have reached after the decisions in *X (Minors)* and *Stovin* v. *Wise*. Control devices may continue to be available to the courts even if the possibility of a duty of care in some cases is admitted. A control device is clearly present in the form of the special pre-tort relationship which existed in each of the *Essex*, *Osman*, and *Elguzouli-Daf* cases, where there were clear elements of reliance and (in the *Essex* case) of undertakings given by the defendant to the plaintiff. In none of these cases could the need to discourage "last resort" litigation realistically be invoked as a reason for defeating the claim.

Stovin v. *Wise* was not a case involving a pre-tort relationship; there was no element of specific reliance and no undertaking given by the defendant to the plaintiff as an individual. Lord Hoffmann's concerns about the implications of joining highway authorities to litigation involving road traffic accidents raise similar issues to those which we have considered under the heading of "last resort" litigation. Was the majority correct, therefore, to reject the possibility of liability in this case? There are in fact several features of *Stovin* v. *Wise* which make it a special case and which could have been used as control devices. As Lord Nicholls of Birkenhead explained in his judgment, the defendant not only had the resources to take the action necessary to remove the hazard, but had failed to do so only because of internal mismanagement, and not because of a decision of policy concerning the allocation of resources. It is true that, in this case, the result of making the highway authority liable would have been to benefit the first defendant's liability insurers. From an economic point of view, however, there may have been nothing wrong with this. As we suggested earlier, where liability follows fault, the workings of the insurance system can ensure that a price is attached to negligent activity (or non-activity), thereby providing incentives for it to be minimised. It is far from clear that the *full* consequences of the accident in *Stovin* v. *Wise* should have been borne by the first defendant's liability insurance, given that the situation of danger in this case was one for which the highway authority was to a certain degree responsible.

In many ways the *X (Minors)* case is the most complex and difficult one from the point of view we are considering here. Nevertheless, it is possible to see how this case, like *Stovin*, could have turned on the presence or absence of fault, rather than being decided on the issue of duty of care (with the result that the issue of fault was never considered). The decision to initiate childcare proceedings (or not) is, in nearly all cases, one involving a high element of professional judgment which the courts could review only with some difficulty. Very similar issues therefore arise as in the context of other situations where the courts must assess whether professional negligence has occurred; and here, as there, it does not seem implausible to suggest that some protection against frivolous claims could have been achieved by the application of the *Bolam*[33] test.

(b) Constitutional factors

(i) *The division of powers between the courts and the executive*

A further category of reasons relates to the division of powers between the courts and the executive when controlling the activities of public bodies. In our view, the current talk of the need to shield public bodies may be going too far in the direction of stating that the only real control is political and not legal. As one

---

[33] *Bolam* v. *Friern Hospital Management Committee* [1957] 1 WLR 582; Markesinis and Deakin, *Tort Law* (4th ed. OUP, 1999), 164–5.

leading public lawyer has observed in his classic textbook,[34] "Public authorities, including ministers of the Crown, enjoy no dispensation from the ordinary law [of the land] This is an important aspect of the rule of law". Echoes of this can be found in Lord Nicholls' dissent in *Stovin* where he reminded us that "The law must recognise the need to protect the public exchequer as well as the private interests".[35] In the light of what will be said below about the validity of the "alternative remedies" argument, one might be forgiven for believing that our judges seem to be losing sight of this aspect of the matter. This is becoming particularly apparent where serious human rights are being violated as a result of this protective stance. All that such statements really betray is the fact that for as long as we do not have a set of morally (if not legally) superior rules, there is as serious risk that human rights values will be sacrificed to traditional tort reasoning. In this context it is interesting to note the contrast with the law in France and Germany where judicial control of public bodies is seen as a legitimate way of additional control and not as a dangerous and unacceptable interference with their decisional powers.

(ii) The existence of alternative remedies

The question of alternative remedies is also relevant in this context. In a few instances, newly invented remedies – for instance an Ombudsman's report – have provided remedies to wronged victims which the tort system could either not produce or might produce after a lengthy and costly litigation. In a handful of other cases, from the group here reviewed, the non-liability rule can be justified by the existence of *truly* alternative and *effective* remedies.[36] We submit, however, that these cases are, in numer-

---

[34] Sir William Wade in Wade and Forsyth, *Adminstrative Law* (7th ed. OUP, 1994), 763.

[35] At 397.

[36] *Olotu* v. *Home Office* [1997] 1 WLR 328, where the remedy of *habeas corpus* was available to the illegally (over)-detained plaintiff and where, one also finds hints, that he might, additionally, have grounds for complaint against those who failed to alert him to his possible remedies. Similarly, in *Hill* v. *Chief*

ical terms, very much the exception.[37] So, how serious are judges when they tell us that a poor, under-privileged and, probably, uneducated citizen who has found himself unjustly held in custody for over three months can bring a successful action for malicious prosecution or misfeasance in public office? It is not just that his social and economic position makes it almost impossible for him even to contemplate taking on the governmental apparatus responsible for his misery – especially in these days of reduced generosity on the part of the Legal Aid Board; it is also that the torts in question have ingredients that make it very difficult to invoke them with any real chance of success. Finally, the availability of purely administrative law type of remedies (e.g., judicial review) are attractive only in theory. In practice, they hardly achieve any (moral) satisfaction; they promote no deterrent function; and they bring about no compensation whatsoever. On the contrary, the conclusion reached in cases such as *Elguzouli* and *Essex County Council*, to the extent that they are (partially) justified by the argument that in all of these instances there is an alternative remedy, can only provoke moral outrage, even among hardened lawyers.

Although this way of testing the validity of "the alternative remedy" argument is not shared (yet?) by the majority of our judges, the *Barrett* decision in the House of Lords provides some signs that not all judges are convinced by the prevailing argumentation we are here criticising. Thus, it is submitted that Lord

Constable of West Yorkshire [1988] 1 WLR 1049 the availability of compensation under the Criminal Injuries Compensation Board obviously weighed on the minds of some of the judges. In this context, however, one must note two things: first, the generosity of the Criminal Injuries Compensation awards are, nowadays, considerably reduced, so the effectiveness of this "alternative" remedy must be looked at very carefully; secondly, in many of the cases reviewed in this book this particular alternative remedy was simply not available.

[37] The Ombudsman's report in the Barlow Clowes affair is, possibly, one of the finest example of such intervention since it led to the government paying out to investors who lost their life saving a sum in the order of £16 million. Several ombudsmen schemes are currently in operation and are described briefly by Professor Peter Cane, *Tort Law and Economic Interests* (2nd ed. OUP, 1996), 366 *ff.*

Hutton was right to go beyond what we are stating, and not merely test the effectiveness of the alternative remedy (as we are suggesting), but assert boldly that "the jurisdiction of the court should not be excluded because of the existence of other measures of complaint".[38] As stated, this argument becomes even stronger when one bears in mind the exceptional paucity of "alternative remedies" asserted to be open to disgruntled plaintiffs. Because of its strong human rights implications, *Elguzouli* is the case that stands out most clearly in our minds.

(c) Inconsistency in the development and application of the law

(i) Bringing the law of tort into disrepute

Conservative lawyers tell us that the imposition of liability in some cases brings the law into disrepute since it insults its dignity. The principle is hardly debatable (although some of the examples given[39] to illustrate its application in practice, e.g., psychiatric injury, are debateable). If the dignity of the law, however, is invoked to condemn decisions which award compensation to victims and which most ordinary folk would regard as deserving, why is the same not happening when the denial of liability produces results which affront most citizens sense of justice? Thus, statements to the effect that one "must not yield to an argument based on the protection of civil liberties" but opt instead for a (subjective) assessment of what serves best the interests of the "whole community"[40] in no way enhance the dignity of the law. Thus, those who regard the dignity of the law as a proper factor for determining the discovery of a duty of care should invoke it with greater consistency than is currently evidenced from their writings.

---

[38] [1999] 3 WLR 79, 114.

[39] For instance, the award of damages to sufferers of psychiatric injury. See Professor Stapleton's feisty "In Defence of Tort" in P Birks (ed.), *The Frontiers of Liability* (OUP, 1994), Vol. 2, 83 *ff.*

[40] *Elguzouli* [1995] 2 WLR 173, 183.

(ii) The misapplication of broad dicta

Broad *dicta*, in striking out actions, are used subsequently to justify judgments in different factual configurations. The policy reasons given in the *Hill* judgments had this effect on almost all cases that followed it. Few subsequent cases picked up the fact that the immunity rule in *Hill* was supportable on the ground that the harm flowed from an omission and not a bad act (as it did in *Elguzouli*). Few of the subsequent cases[41] also failed to explore the reality that their facts, unlike those of *Hill*, arguably involved mistakes made in the operational areas of police activities and not in the traditionally excluded area of policy. To the extent that this proves convincing – and, of course, in legal matters there is always room for argument – it suggests that the "preservation of scarce resources argument", first enunciated in *Hill*, has ruled the day and has in practice led to a blanket immunity. Thus, many will have been struck by the way the *Bedfordshire* pronouncements were used, almost verbatim, to strike out the parents' claims in the *Essex* case. What remedy was available to them, either as aggrieved parents or aggrieved ratepayers, against their local authority? Some lawyers may also be unhappy with the fact that the "fair, just and reasonable" requirement was introduced in these cases and utilised as a further means of limiting liability. The extension in *Marc Rich* by a divided House of Lords of such an "uncomfortably loose test for the existence of a legal duty"[42] from cases concerning pure economic loss to a case involving a property damage to a vessel is debatable. But it is literally unjustified, if not also unjustifiable, where abhorrent invasions incidents, such as those found in the *Essex* case, are at issue. Thus, it can be argued that in their recent judgments our courts have taken the rationale of *Hill* too far, moving from a position which was understandable, perhaps even justifiable, to one which even hardened lawyers may find difficult to accept.

[41] As, for instance, *Alexandrou* v. *Oxford* [1993] 4 All ER 328; *Osman* v. *Ferguson* [1993] 4 All ER 344; *Ancell* v. *McDermott* [1993] 4 All ER 355.

[42] The words belong to Lord Nicholls in *Stovin* v. *Wise* [1996] 3 WLR 38,8 396.

(iii) Inconsistency in the treatment of professionals

A further result of the five cases we are considering here is a
marked difference in the treatment of different categories of professionals. For instance, why are we willing to second-guess doctors but not willing to attempt the same with local authority
officials? Is it because the courts are better equipped to perform
the former rather than the latter task? Is it because we are more
anxious to protect the anonymous civil servant from the epony-
mous doctor? Or is it because insurance practices work differently in the one case but not in the other? The same objections
apply to the other argument advanced in favour of police and
local authority immunity: liability would make them more timid
and more hesitant to act. But why are actions against local
authorities or the police any more likely to make them hesitant
than malpractice actions made doctors over-defensive? (The
contrary assertion, although often made, has never, to our
knowledge, been proved empirically.) Until reliable answers are
given to the above questions, one is thus bound to feel that the
law treats the public body more leniently than the private
defender. Even those who have favoured immunity in our cases
have not advocated such a different treatment between public
and private bodies.[43]

(d) Tort law and human rights

A further consequence of these decisions is the fact that our
present law is bound to create friction with, at first instance, the
Court in Strasbourg and, in due course, with our own human
rights legislation. Lord Justice Steyn admitted as much in his
Elguzouli judgment; and if we share the fear that such a conflict
is looming ahead, we should do our uttermost to avoid it. Our
submission has, all along, been that such conflict will be avoided
only if recourse to the notion of duty of care, as the device that
produces blanket immunities, is abandoned. As stated, calls for

---

[43] "In the case of positive acts . . . the liability of a public authority in tort is
in principle the same as that of a private person but may be *restricted* by its statutory powers and duties.' *Stovin* v. *Wise* [1996] 3 WLR 388, 409.

degrading the use of this device in our law of torts are as old as the concept itself; but the need to do something about this is now becoming a matter of practical necessity and is no longer merely a topic fit for academic speculation. If such a change would take too bold a move, then our judges could, at least, make a start, by downgrading the requirement of fair, just and reasonable which they – wrongly in our view – extended to physical harms, and which has provided the entry point for so many of these conservative policies. The "fair, just and reasonable" device is young in age and can thus be remoulded more easily than the cardinal concept itself.

In this context, we must also ask the following, basic question: what is the state trying to achieve in all these cases? In general and abstract terms the answer must be that it is acting in a regulatory or supervisory function. Now, in some of the cases that can be brought under this broad heading, one could argue that the purpose of the norms which govern the regulatory function is to ensure that the (appropriate) rules laid down by primary or delegated legislation are observed by those who have to apply them. Such a definition could, for instance, be used to justify the non-liability rule reached in *Yuen Kun Yeu* v. *Attorney-General for Hong Kong*[44] where the regulatory regime concerned financial services and pension. Such an explanation/justification of the *Yeun Kun Yeu* case is not, of course, compelling in any legal or logical sense. We can see this both from studying other developed systems which have not followed this approach[45] but we can also see it from the equally noteworthy fact that our system, as well, has ignored this "logic" of non-compensation by opting for a completely different solution *where public pressure is both large and organised.*[46] It does have the merit of not sharing the

[44] [1988] AC 175.

[45] E.g., the German system where the view taken by the courts is that state supervision of banking not only serves the public weal but also the interests of individual investors. Thus, see Markesinis, *The German Law of Obligations*, Vol. II, *The Law of Torts* (3rd ed. OUP, 1997), 905 (with reference to BGHZ 68, 142).

[46] The Barlow Clowes affair offers an illustration of the point since £150 mil-

whole edifice of tort law but justifying a departure only where it can be argued that the primary aim of the regulatory function is to act in the interests of a weaker section of society. The *Bedfordshire*, *Barrett* and *Essex* cases could thus very plausibly be brought under this heading since here, as Professor John Bell, among others, has argued, "the idea of the protective norm suggests that [the state] should be liable to [those vulnerable people] for its failure to live up to expectations".[47] There is, in other words, plenty of room to argue that some of the cases we have encountered in this book can lay a strong claim to being decided differently than they have done thus far. Incidentally, in order to avoid frightening Germanophobes, we have so far deliberately spoken of the "scope of the norm" rather than the well-known German term of *Normzweck. But terms do not really matter.* What matters, instead, is the fact that this way of analysing legal problems was invented almost simultaneously (in the late-twenties) in Germany by Ernest Rabel, and in the United States by Leon Green. That, however, is only a detail!

Finally, we cite as a further reason the argument that can be culled from the experience of other, major, European legal systems. In the law of those countries we find a legal position, which casts grave doubts on the reality of the fears advanced by those who oppose the introduction of the tort rules in this part of the law. Such a different case law, unaccompanied by the apocalyptic consequences which the English detractors of tort law so often invoke, merits at least a closer study in order to discover why solutions which are deemed so unworkable in England have worked in France and Germany.

lion was, apparently, paid out to those who suffered from the regulatory failure in that case. On this, see Gregory and Drewry, "Barlow Clowes and the Ombudsman" [1991] *PL* 192, 408. I The fact that the payment in that instance was *ex gratia* does not affect the argument in the text above.

[47] "Government Liability in Tort", *National Journal of Constitutional Law* 85, 101.

2. More doubts from abroad.[48] *Osman* v. *UK* and the growing impact of human rights law on English tort law

The *Hill* rule, achieving as it does immunity for the police through the use of the notion of duty of care, can, *in practice if not strictly speaking in theory*, be seen as conferring "a blanket immunity on the police for their acts and omissions during the investigation and suppression of crime". Until the Strasbourg judgment in *Osman* approached it from a different perspective no one, to our knowledge, had in this country even considered the possibility that such a blanket exclusion of liability could amount to a denial of justice for the plaintiff/victim who has his claim rejected through the use of the notion of duty of care. On the contrary, the case was seen as a simple example of a striking out action. As we shall see, the Strasbourg Court – with the concurrence of the English judge – did not share this optic at all but, on the contrary, took the view (in para. 139 of its judgment) that:

> "the applicants must be taken to have a right, derived from the law of negligence, to seek *an adjudication*[49] on the admissibility and merits of an arguable claim. . ."

In the Court's view, the question of whether the restriction of that right (to have one's case heard) was compatible with Article 6 (1) of the European Convention on Human Rights was to be determined later.

The tragic case that provoked this recourse to the Strasbourg

---

[48] Andenas and Fairgrieve also point out the potential assistance that English law may derive from Community law. Thus, see "Sufficiently Serious? Judicial Restraint in Tortious Liability of Public Authorities and the European Influence" in Mads Andenas (ed.), *English Public law and the Common Law of Europe*, ch. 14. In the introductory chapter to the book the editor also rightly questions (at 3) whether the English courts will, in the long run, be able to operate two sets of rules, two types of remedies and two forms of reasoning "depending on whether the administrative action is based on a Community law measure or not".

[49] Our emphasis.

court was *Osman* v. *Ferguson*.[50] The case involved a school-teacher who, in 1987, developed an "unhealthy" obsession with one of his young charges.[51] Both the boy, who rejected these advances, and his parents, complained to the school and its head teacher. This led to a number of interviews with the teacher who became increasingly hostile and engaged in a series of menacing acts affecting the young boy's family. The police, who had been informed of the teacher's behaviour, apparently remained inactive, even after it became known that the dejected and depressed teacher "threatened to do a Hungerford".[52] A year later, as the acts of criminal violence increased, the police were, apparently, putting together a file with a view to prosecuting the mentally deranged teacher. But, alas, he acted first, by killing the father and injuring the boy's brother. The judge at first instance refused to strike out the plaintiff's action; but his decision was reversed by the Court of Appeal which relied on the *Hill* ruling even though in this case the proximity factor, contested in *Hill*, was found to exist in favour of the plaintiff. The Strasbourg Court, seized of the dispute, recently held[53] that such blanket immunities may "amount to an unjustifiable restriction of an applicant's right to have a determination on the merits of his or

[50] [1993] 4 All ER 344.

[51] That over twelve years have been required to lapse before a semblance of justice could be achieved in this case is, itself, a serious condemnation of our system. It is also a tangible example of how the repatriation of human rights by our recent Human Rights Act should save litigants' time and the country the embarrassment of being told that its system of justice is deficient by a foreign court. But that is another matter!

[52] In 1987 Hungerford became the scene of a massacre in which a gunman burst into a school, killed sixteen persons and then committed suicide. The exact words used by the assailant in this case were the subject of some dispute.

[53] *Osman* v. *UK* (1998) *The Times*, 5 November (No. 87/1997/871/1083). In our discussion we say nothing about the Court's use of Article 6 to justify its intervention in this case, partly because of lack of space but mainly because we do not feel that it is right to distract the reader's attention from the fact that this decision of the Grand Chamber, although not technically binding upon English courts, is likely to have an important impact upon our law. This impact is likely to be even greater if, as expected, Strasbourg follows the same path when it pronounces on the *Bedfordshire* case now pending before it.

her claim against the police in deserving cases". Thus, the Court ruled that all the considerations relevant to the complainant's claim should also "be examined on the merits and *not automatically excluded*[54] by the application of a rule which amounted to the grant of an immunity to the police". This led to a (unanimous) decision that in the instant case the exclusionary rule (in *Hill*) "constituted a disproportionate restriction on the applicants' right of access to a court and for that reason there had been a violation of Article 6 (1) of the Convention".

As already indicated, the significance of the decision just described goes far beyond its immediate facts. First, it is likely – ulimtately, if not immediately – to provide a serious and, in accordance with what we have said above, well-deserved blow to the use of the notion of duty of care as a (blunt) device for effectively preventing damage claims against public bodies in general (and not just the police). If this leads to an increase in litigation, as the supporters of the status quo will argue, we submit that such an increase will be of a short duration (and could be further curbed by the award of small amounts, at any rate for non-pecuniary headings of damage). In support of this prediction we invoke the many instances (trespassers, liability for negligent references, psychiatric injury, etc.) found in our modern tort law where the opening of the floodgates was predicted – both in England and the United States (but did not materialise) – every time an effort was made to liberalise or modernise our tort rules.

Secondly, we feel that the danger of frivolous claims being brought will also prove confinable through the use of other legal devices available to our courts including, of course, the burden of costly litigation and, as we suggested, the award of modest damages for the non-pecuniary parts of any such claims. In this context one must note the, as yet, unknown effect which the restriction of legal aid will have on the incidents of litigation. Moreover, we feel that even if its takes some time to achieve this type of litigation equilibrium, any temporary uncertainty that may ensue will be considered by many to be a small price to pay

[54] Our emphasis.

in exchange for ensuring that justice is not only done, but is also seen to be done.

Thirdly, we remind readers that other such cases are currently pending before the Strasbourg court. If the Strasbourg court follows its approach in *Osman* in cases such as *X* v. *Bedfordshire County Council* currently before it, it will bring about a significant rethinking in English tort doctrine. The outrageous facts of the *Osman* case (and, indeed, other cases such as *Elguzouli* and *Essex*) suggest that some of our judges, in their current "cerebral" mode, may be sacrificing traditional tort aims such as justice, deterrence and compensation to the altar of prudent management of admittedly scarce resources. The important point made in this book is that the current English approach to these problems is not the only realistic one available to any court of justice. The foreign experience, especially in Germany and France, suggests that other alternatives may merit more consideration, especially in the light of the fact that Europe is sending signals which we simply cannot *wholly* ignore. But our predictions to what may follow *Osman* are subject to the usual *caveat* that it is dangerous to prophecy about the future and, in any event, are less relevant for present purposes. What is more significant is to say a few words about the reactions that have thus far appeared with regard to the *Osman* case. Three, in our view, stand out for comment.

The first can be dealt with briefly since its discussion does not really pertain to this work but to those which specialise in the jurisprudence of the Strasbourg Court. It is based on a straightforward reading of the text of Article 6(1) of the Convention which provides that, "In the determination of his civil rights and obligations . . . everyone is entitled to a fair and public hearing . . .". As Lord Browne Wilkinson quite rightly put it:[55]

> "this would seem to require that the applicant has, under the local law, a right (right A) enforceable in the local court. Under Article 6 he is given as a separate right (right B) a right of access to the local courts to assert right A being a separate, free standing right. Thus

---

[55] *Barrett* v. *Enfield London Borough Council* [1999] 3 WLR 79, 84.

one would assume that right A would consist of, for example, a contractual right or a tortious right not to be negligently injured. If a person is prevented from enforcing those rights that is not an infringement of right A but an infringement of right B i.e. the right of access to court."

Lord Browne-Wilkinson then went on to state that, as far as he could see, *Osman* did not say that but, effectively, created a new right A for the plaintiff. His Lordship is, we submit, correct on this point,[56] with the result that the Strasbourg Court could be accused of having indulged in an interpretation of Article 6(1) of the Convention which is both novel and objectionable.

"Novel" we think it is, although in fairness it could also be seen as a continuation of a conscious decision to adopt a creative approach towards Article 6 which goes back at least until the *Golder*[57] decision of the same Court and, in our view, further expanded in the *Fayed* case.[58] But is it also "objectionable"? This brings us to the other two objections which, we indicated earlier, have already been levelled against *Osman*. Both are interrelated, and we shall look at them only to the extent that is necessary for the purposes of this book.

---

[56] Subject, we think, to the *caveat* that the right envisaged by the Court was, in essence, only a right to have whatever claim the plaintiff might have according to the law of torts adjudicated and not summarily (and routinely) dismissed in a striking out action. We read Lord Browne-Wilkinson's judgment in *Barrett* in the same light, since the learned Law Lord was anxious to say that in some instances such cases should be heard and this can only imply that there is an underlying basic right. We further see this as an important feature of the case since, in proximity terms, the *Osman* case differed from *Hill*.

[57] *Golder* v. *UK* (1975) EHRR 524.

[58] *Fayed* v. *UK* (1994) 18 EHRR 393 where, interestingly, the court said (para. 65):

"it would not be consistent with the rule of law in a democratic society or with the basic principle underlying Article 6(1) – namely that civil claims must be capable of being submitted to a judge for adjudication – if, for example, a State could, without restraint or control by the Convention enforcement bodies, remove from the jurisdiction of the courts a whole range of civil claims or confer immunities for civil liability on large groups or categories of persons . . ."

The prime objection would seem to be that Strasbourg cannot create *new*[59] rights for the United Kingdom; or, to put it differently, it should be forced to respect the fact that this role belongs to the United Kingdom Parliament and courts. In principle, this is certainly correct, especially if we interpret the doctrine of parliamentary sovereignty in a very literal fashion. However, few would say that such an approach would nowadays tally with realities; and the reality we have in mind is the growing influence that human rights values are having on our law. This reality, in our view, means that the new human rights environment[60] may, on occasion, affect even the powers of the national legislator (or courts) to delimit the existence and contents of nationally recognised rights. Imagine, thus, the following series of examples.

Imagine first if Parliament were to pass a law saying that British Jews, because of their race, had no civic rights. Would such an enactment, even assuming that it surmounted the obvious political obstacles which would be put in its way, escape the control of the European Court (even if it had that of a British court)? Could anyone dare to argue that national law recognised no rights and thus could bar such persons from going to courts? The answer must surely be "no" for the simple reason that the older doctrine of parliamentary sovereignty would have to yield to the growing influence that human rights law – both of the indigenous and imported variety – has on English law. In short, human rights will no longer tolerate crude race discrimination. A British Jew who thus found himself defeated by an English court would, undoubtedly, be able to complain that his Convention rights had been violated.

[59] See P. Craig and D. Fairgrieve, "Barrett, Negligence and Discretionary Powers" – unpublished paper delivered at a conference held at Kings College, London, on August 2nd, 1999.

[60] The impact of this new human rights (political) environment on traditional concepts of law – national and international – can be seen by looking at how the recent events in Yugoslavia/Kosovo have been handled from the point of view of public international law. The recent *Pinochet* rulings by the House of Lords can also be seen as reflecting a new appreciation of the impact of human rights on hitherto differently understood rules of law.

Now let us move a scale down and imagine another example, namely that a law was passed allowing only men to hold the office of Prime Minster of the United Kingdom. Such legislation would give no such right to a woman; but no English or Strasbourg Court would uphold it since, once again, it would run counter to another set of human rights values which has, in relatively recent times, become acceptable, and that is the equality between sexes. Human rights values would thus, once again, override internal legislation; and we assume that if an English court failed to grant a woman complainant an appropriate remedy on the grounds that the English Parliament recognised her no such right could, again, be overturned by Strasbourg on a number of grounds including violation of Article 6(1).

Let us finally move a notch further down and closer to the facts of the *Osman* case. Suppose that an English statute (or the courts) had proclaimed that a person who had suffered loss as a result of a careless act or omission of a statutory body was *never* to be allowed to seek redress before a court of law. Would such an enactment escape the control of the Strasbourg Court on the ground that no claim was recognised by English law? All kinds of human rights reasons could be invoked to argue in favour of a negative answer, and we think this is precisely why Lord Brown-Wilkinson, in his opinion in *Barrett*, stressed over and over again that "I find it impossible to say that all careless acts or omissions of a local authority in relation to a child in its care are not actionable".[61] However if that is what he *said*, that is not what he and his colleagues have being doing in practice in *X* v. *Bedfordshire County Council*, *Osman*, *Elgozouli*, *Barrett*, and in so many other cases. In a series of cases, *which range over a very wide area of activities of different types of statutory bodies*, they have *effectively* been denying even to consider the issue of liability. Indeed, some leading judges (such as Lord Woolf in the Court of Appeal in *Barrett*[62]) have been particularly honest to admit that such actions will very rarely succeed in practice. In the light

[61] [1993] 3 WLR 79, 82.
[62] [1998] QB 367.

of this *practice*, is it really surprising that the Strasbourg Court took the view that a device of national law – the duty of care – which in the vast majority of cases blocks a litigant from having the merits of his case tested in court, leads to a denial of access to a court of law under Article 6(1) of the Convention? We submit that invoking the striking out practice as a defence and arguing that the Strasbourg Court misunderstood its aims is not really very convincing. For judges who begin, as the Strasbourg judges do, with the kind of liberal and philosophical assumptions we have tried to describe in this book, this way of looking at things is unreasonable. More importantly, their concerns, if not their methodology, are bound also to influence the English approach. Indeed, less than one year after Osman was decided, it is already having some effect on English courts if one is to judge not simply by the result in *Barrett* but, just as importantly, the Senior Law Lord's desire to stress that a striking out action would not be – and should not be seen to be – a real and total block to having one's case tested before a court. How exactly the English courts will, in the end, square this position with the traditional use they have made of the duty concept remains to be seen. One can only foresee a compromise; but what comes out of such a compromise will undoubtedly have affected the traditional use and role of the notion of duty of care.

Which brings us to the last accusation hurled at *Osman*, no doubt in order to take it out of the human rights arena and avoid the above-mentioned reactions. This came from Lord Hoffmann who, writing extra-judicially, tried to debase *Osman* even further by arguing that it was not really a human rights case at all. The learned Law Lord thus tried to explain *Osman* as being a case that involved no civil rights issues whatsoever but, merely, "[dealt] with the substantive civil law right to financial compensation for not receiving the benefit of a social service"[63] – in this case proper policing of a particular community. This, in turn, made it easier for him to voice the concern (already addressed) that the *Osman* decision:

[63] "Human Rights and the House of Lords" (1999) 62 *MLR* 159, 166.

"challenge[es] the autonomy of the courts and indeed the Parliament of the United Kingdom to deal with what are *essentially social welfare questions involving budgetry limits and efficent public administration.*"[64]

Yet, as we have suggested time and again in this book, nothing could have been further from the minds of the judges in *Osman* who were, instead, challenging the blanket immunity which results in practice from the utilisation of the notion of duty of care, and doing this against a philosophical background which gives judges the right to control the administration in all its emanations. In their view, such an absolute and unchallengable way of stopping the courts from even investigating the merits of a case was unacceptable insofar as it represented an interference with Article 6 rights as understood by the Court in its most recent jurisprudence. Thus, to present the case as "essentially involving welfare questions and budgetary limits" not only does injustice to the Strasbourg Court; it also prevents English lawyers from questioning the real consequences that flow from such open-ended and blunt notions as that of "duty of care" when used in cases such as these.

[64] Ibid, 164 (emphasis added).

4
Comparative Conclusions

As stated at the beginning of Chapter one, the tortious liability of statutory bodies has, in England and throughout this century, been the subject of only three monographs, erudite but on the whole brief, and one or two articles which one could be tempted to describe as feisty in style but not very convincing in substance. Surely such a state of affairs can no longer be tolerated. What cries out for a change and justifies further studies of this subject is first and foremost the change in political philosophy, which has lead to a proliferation of statutory bodies charged with ever-growing powers that can affect our lives. Just as important are three other phenomena.

First, whether one likes it or not, it is a fact that many statutory bodies, including the police and local welfare services, are no longer seen as having a totally unblemished record. On the contrary, hardly a day goes by without the national press reporting some error committed by those bodies, often entailing considerably sad consequences. Secondly, on the more technical, legal side, there is a growing awareness that topics such as ours can no longer be studied within the insular settings of one single legal system. This is not only the result of comparatists urging their national colleagues to look abroad for inspiration; it is mainly due to the growing impact that the two European courts – in Luxemburgh and Strasbourg – are having on the national legal systems of most of Europe. Finally, one could mention the growing belief that the discovery of the best answer to the kind of problems which we have been discussing in this book can be facilitated by an interdisciplinary approach and should no longer be left to lawyers acting on their own and in isolation from other disciplines, especially that of economics. However, the complexity of the problems we have alluded to also means that one must accept from the very outset that, while few of our readers would question the validity of the above assertions, not all will share the way we have used these assumptions. We are even more conscious of the fact that not all of our readers will welcome our proposed remedies to the underlying problem which we see as a tendency to slide all too easily into the non-liability option. This tendency could not have been expressed more graphically than when Lord Hoffmann, using computer terminology, argued that "The default position is [that there is no entitlement to compensation from the person who has caused the harm]".[1]

Undeniably, there is something of a missionary in every academic. Understandably, therefore, we would be happy if the English courts were willing to shift their current position in the direction of our own beliefs. Yet, in writing this book, converting others to our preferred solutions has not been our main aim. What we have tried to do instead is bring together our combined knowledge on this subject and to present it in a form that might be digestible to English judges, who sometimes give the impression of being removed from the concerns of ordinary citizens. We feel this to be so when the merits or demerits of cases such as *Bedfordshire*,[2] *Essex*,[3] and *Elguzouli*[4] seem to be submerged in entangled distinctions (such as that between policy and operational decisions) on which even the judges, themselves, seem unable to agree.[5] But there is another reason for targeting judges; and since it has been explained by the first of us on so

---

[1] *Stovin* v. *Wise* [1996] 3 WLR 388, 411.

[2] *X (Minors)* v. *Bedfordshire County Council* [1994] 2 WLR 554.

[3] *W* v. *Essex County Council*.

[4] *Elgozouli-Daf* v. *Commissioner of Police of the Metropolis* [1995] 2 WLR 173.

[5] Some judges admit as much themsleves. Thus, see Lord Brown Wilkinson's extra-judicial observation in "The X case: Implication for Educational Lawyers. An Address by Lord Browne Wilkinson" (1996) *Education Law Association*, 3. (We are grateful to Dr Mads Andenas, of King's College, London, for bringing this unpublished paper to our attention.) We are similarly not convinced that the more modern discussion about "justiciability" will fare any better; but we leave this to administrative lawyers to sort out for themselves.

many occasions,[6] we feel that it would be wasting valuable space to elaborate on the basic belief on which this theory is based. Quite simply, it is our shared belief that the best way to serve our subject – comparative law and methodology – is to try to devise a method that makes it useful to those who *practice* law – be they judges or practitioners. As already stated, this book is thus as much a study in comparative methodology as it is an attempt to describe some basic rules about foreign – mainly French and German – law and suggest that English lawyers may be able to draw some lessons from them. A second, though no less important, consequence of our efforts is to encourage a greater co-operation between the academic and practising side of our profession.

Let us end the book, therefore, as we started it, namely with a few thoughts about comparative methodology.

What our survey shows is that however much one tries to narrow one's focus in order to sharpen it – and we did this by looking only at five, litigated, factual configurations – one cannot understand the working of legal rules unless one ultimately sees them within their wider setting. Thus, by narrowing our discussion to five concrete situations we could show that the problems were the same in all of our three models. However, we also quickly became aware that characterisation and appraisal of the foreign solutions was impossible without seeing them within their wider socio-legal context. The first lesson was thus that in any comparative study one must start by dispelling the instinctive fears one feels about "foreign law"; and the best way of doing this is often by presenting one's reader with narrow (and thus manageable) factually equivalent situations. Once this is done, however, one should then proceed to broaden the understanding of one's audience by analysing the particular solutions within the wider political and economic context of the foreign country being examined. If the socio-economic and cultural setting is broadly similar between the systems compared, one can then take the third and last step and attempt to draw conclusions

[6] His views can be found in a collection of essays published under the title *Foreign Law and Comparative methodology: A Subject and a Thesis* (Oxford, Hart 1998).

from the foreign system with a greater degree of confidence than one otherwise might have had without this broader understanding. In our case this meant (a) looking at the facts of the cases chosen as examples and studying their solutions within the context of the *political* philosophy which prevails in the country whose system is being studied, and (b) studying them in conjunction with other, related *legal* rules.

Attempting (a) was in one sense easier than (b). For (a) confirms a point made not long ago by Professor John Bell (among others), namely that "European administrative law traditions remain very national".[7] In particular, it could be argued that the current, very generous position adopted by the French legal system is understood better if seen within the context of the political philosophy that has dominated the thinking of French governments during the last twenty years or so. This has been distinctly more "left" than that found in both England and Germany during the comparable period of time. This observation must be coupled with a parallel sociological evolution found, again, most strongly in France and known as the idea of the *"société assurantielle"* (risk socialisation). These phenomena in combination have, undoubtedly, taken "consumerism" – perhaps the single most important legal theme of this century – to new heights *and new areas*. Of these two phrases, "new areas" is, for our purposes, the most significant. For we all know how, during the last thirty years or so, the consumer movement has affected *private* law in all three countries studied here, and has

[7] "Mechanisms for Cross-fertilisation of Administrative Law in Europe" in Beatson and Tridimis (eds), *New Directions in European Public Law* (Oxford, Hart, 1998), 147. However, this perfectly valid observation does not prevent Professor Bell asserting "that international interaction and collaboration at a practical and an academic level has and will continue to shape the development of specific national traditions" (ibid., 147). In his view, such a cross-fertilisation is likely to be at its strongest in the area of "values" rather than "procedures". One must further note that scholars have already begun examining how cross-fertilisation and convergence of solutions can be encouraged even further. Thus, see Eivind Smith, "Give and Take: Cross-fertilisation of Concentps in Consitutional Law", and John F Allison, "Transplanation and Cross-Fertilisation" in Beatson and Tridimas (eds), *op. cit.*, chs 8 and 12 respectively.

done so in a fairly radical but similar manner. This, after all, is the period that saw the introduction in most European systems of similar hire-purchase and money-lending legislation, as well as analogous statutes protecting consumers from excessively rigorous exemption clauses or defective products or services. Cardinal notions of the liberal doctrine of contract were, for better or for worse – this is not our concern here – thus affected in a very significant manner. However, the little that has been said about French law on our subject shows that French administrative courts took the spirit of consumerism very much to heart and, as a result, shaped a philosophy and a set of solutions which, we hazard the guess, most English judges would regard as vague if not, arguably, dubious. To the extent that we are right in second-guessing their reaction to French politcal philosophy, we suspect that French law is unlikely to hold out much appeal immediately, at any rate to *practising* English lawyers. Yet, before one jumps to the other extreme and dismisses French law as completely irrelevant, one must also ask oneself two further questions.

The first, as already hinted, is philosophical. French administrative judges begin with the assumption that it is essentially unfair to impose on ordinary persons the burden of administration activities, which are achieved for the benefit of the whole of society. This factor seems, with some notable exceptions,[8] to be missing almost completely from the mental calculations made by English judges. However, it is not entirely without merit. The French experience (and literature) thus deserve – at the very least – some consideration by the English side. We have already given instances – *Elguzouli*, *Essex* and *Bedfordshire* – where we feel this factor is at its strongest. Yet, undeniably, it has been ignored by the English courts.

The second observation that is justified by looking at French administrative practices is something of a paradox. Thus, we see that despite the generous predisposition French law shows

---

[8] Lord Bingham's reasoning in the Court of Appeal in *X* v. *Bedfordshire County Council* strikes us as an opposite illustration which this kind of thinking may also attract supporters in England.

towards the kinds of claims considered in this book, it has, nonetheless, managed to work. What we mean by this is that (a) the incidents of litigation remain limited; (b) the state, in all its forms and emanations, has not literally collapsed under the kind of economic pressures which instil such fear in the heart of Lord Hoffmann; and (c) academic (or intellectual) complaints against this state of affairs are neither loud nor numerous. How can all this be explained?

To such a question we readily admit that we have not been able to provide *conclusive and empirically* supported answers. We do not, however, believe that this book, which raises more questions than it can answer, has, for this reason, failed its purpose. First and foremost, making people think and consider is one of the primary tasks academics must perform. Additionally, however, we have also tried to understand what we found in the foreign systems and answer our own queries. Thus, where no obvious answers were to be found in the area of our *immediate* enquiry, we turned our attention to related areas of the law as a possible source of explanation. This approach explains our previously made statement that the operation of a particular rule can often be understood by studying some other set of norms, not always found in the same area or even branch of the law. To put it differently: the need to interrelate the various parts of whatever legal systems one is studying became, once again, very obvious. In this search we believe that we may have stumbled upon some interesting data which could be used as a source of inspiration for our system should it ever decide to re-orient itself in the way we are advocating.

For a brief moment we thus wondered whether the real answer to the French liability rule thus lay in the parsimonious tendencies of the French courts, already alluded to in our text, in fixing levels of monetary awards. Thus, although the condemnation of a statutory body could provide "satisfaction" for the aggrieved party (and also remain consistent with the philosophical tendencies alluded to above), a very low level of damages would not entail the economic ruination of the said statutory body. This, of course, is not an solution which would go down well with all English lawyers, some of whom would, we suspect rightly, not feel happy immitating a rule which encouraged delay in the settling of disputes and provoked high transaction costs for the sake of a token award amounting to a "rap on the knuckle" of a "misbehaving" authority. Be that as it may, this could still have been a (theoretical) explanation of sorts, accounting for the differences between these two systems and explaning why the French local authorities have not collapsed under the pressure of a generous liability rule.

Unfortunately, the paucity of available *empirical* data documenting the levels of French awards made such an explanation tentative though not implausible.[9] Moreover, the "comfort factor" provided by this "intuition" was reduced further by the growing awareness, confirmed by consulting practising lawyers, that the level of damages is rising.[10] Thus, the only points on which there seemed to be no doubt were three: first, the philosophical belief of French administrative judges that such losses should be born by the community since the activities that caused

---

[9] Those involved in transnational litigation know how important it is to back the widely held belief that European levels of damages are lower than, say, US levels with hard evidence. But the real crux of the matter lies in proving *how much lower* they are; and this is very difficult to do even in straightforward accident cases, which thus far have received the greatest attention.

[10] Thus, not only was the original aversion of the administrative law judges to award "moral damages" (i.e., non-pecuniary damages) overcome, the amounts given under this heading have increased progressively from a derogatory FF 2,000 or 3,000 (£30 at 1999 rates of exchange) in the 1960s (see, for instance, Conseil d' Etat, 24 novembre 1961, *Recueil des arrêts du Conseil d' Etat*, 661) to over FF 50,000 (i.e., £5,000) in the late 1980s (Conseil d' Etat, 23 septembre 1987, *Recueil des arrêts du Conseil d' Etat*, 290), and then jumped to FF 2,000,000 (i.e., £200,000) in the most recent AIDS contamination cases (Conseil d' Etat, 9 avril 1993, *Recueil des arrêts du Conseil d' Etat*, 110). These figures may be lower than those that could be awarded by English courts, but they are no longer derogatory. Taken together with the German awards, they may also hold out a lesson for English courts. Incidentally, AIDS-related suits, brought against state hospitals (or state blood-transfusion agencies) and thus litigated before admisnitrative courts, provoked an increase in monetary awards for non-pecuniary damages all over Europe. Examples are given by von Bar, "Schmerzensgeld in Europa" (1999) *Festschrift für Erwin Deutsch zum 70. Geburstag*, 27 *ff.*

them were carried out in the interests of the same community; secondly, the explanation that the French system "worked" solely because of the derisory measure of its damages was, if ever true, no longer sustainable; and, thirdly, that a proper evaluation of the economic thinking behind French judgments was impossible simply because so little of it appeared in any of the official or semi-official records. (Again, however, we note that there was a general debate about economic and insurance matters when the decision was taken to widen the liability of state hospitals.)

In some respects the position in Germany seemed more reassuring for our emerging conclusions, since the difficulties described above in connection with French law seemed to be attenuated. Thus, our German colleague was able to produce evidence of elaborate and long-standing discussions concerning the economic consequences of the liability rule, *some of it empirical in nature*. Indeed, what is so interesting about these German debates is that they have, in essence, preceded the current English discussions by about one hundred years and have now moved on to different levels which, philosophically, come closer to the French model than the English. Secondly, we noted that many of the policy arguments advanced in England against the imposition of liability had, again, been considered in Germany and had been rejected, in some cases many years ago. Thirdly, we noted that in this system, too, the measure of damages provides no justification of the liability rule since, even though damages are, undoubtedly, modest when it comes to the *non-pecuniary* part of the award[11] – what Germans call damages

[11] See, for instance OLG Oldenburg VersR 1991, 305, where the plaintiff's claim for 100,000 DM for being illegally incarcerated for five days was reduced from 100,000 DM to 5,000 DM – at todays exchange rate roughly the equivalent of £1,700. Incidentally, though this figure is miniscule by comparison to sums given in the USA for these kind of torts, it is not much out of line of English awards made around the same time. Thus, see *Bishop* v. *Metropolitan Police Commissioner & others* (1989) *The Times*, 5 December (£1,500 for malicious prosecution); *Barnes* v. *Commissioner of Police for the Metropolis* (1992) L.A.G., 14 (£2,500 for false imprisonment); *Linton* v. *E. J. Parkinson & Son Ltd*, 11 May 1989 (£2,900: industrial tribunal award for discrimination). In *Noone* v. *N. W. Thames RHA* (1992) 41 EOR 20, the Court of Appeal suggested

which aim to provide "satisfaction" (*Genuugtung*) not "compensation to the victim" – the levels of compensation provided for provable economic losses can be substantial and, if anything, higher than the French.[12] If Lord Hoffmann's reasoning were right, the German liability rules would have brought in their wake considerable economic difficulties for all German statutory bodies subject to them. Yet nothing of the sort has happened. On the contrary, officially commissioned statistics have shown that the financial burden of state liability (including all causes of action, not just breach of official duty) amounted to only 0.015% of the total budget. Once again, therefore, one is forced to doubt the validity of the English fears or, at the very least, set them aside *until some figures can be produced to support them.*

These findings thus obliged us to seek explanations for the German results elsewhere. Our conclusion is that the system works, and there is no pressure to alter its basic structure. Our explanation is (tentatively) based on the *cumulative* effect of the following reasons: (a) insurance provides a workable framework; (b) liability makes civil servants more careful; (c) where the cost is, indeed, substantial, it is thought that it is right and proper to spread it among the community to which the statutory authority belongs; and (d) finally, although the level of damages is not derisory, judges have never allowed it to reach the exorbitant levels that, say, US tort awards can reach. The *Bedfordshire* and *Essex* type of cases would seem to fall neatly within the above parameters; and the wider German thinking behind such an approach would, it seems, approximate the French philosophical stance mentioned above. Once again, however, we nourish no illusion that all our readers will agree with such an analysis. As such, we are putting forward these thoughts for further

that the maximum award for injured feelings in such cases should be £3,000 (though some later cases have exceeded double this amount).

[12] *Cf.* For example the German equivalent to *Elguzouli* – BGH of 16 October 1997, NJW 1998, 751 – where the damages claimed for pecuniary losses amounted to over DM 160,990, or approximately £55,000: BGH NJW 1971, 751–52. Similarly, in the German equivalent to *Essex* – OLG Hamm, FamRZ 1993, 704 – where the adoptive parents of an unhealthy child who were granted the costs of looking after the child for life.

consideration by scholars who might be able and willing to test their validity *with the aid of further empirical data.* We feel confident, however, that our preliminary findings (or suggestions) cannot be rebutted merely by putting forward judicial intuitions. We consider this "request" to be entirely consistent with our belief that some areas of the law are best studied in an interdisciplinary way and cannot be handled properly through black-letter law concepts alone. We also feel that the English legal aid system, with its merit-testing procedures and financial thresholds is, if anything, even more likely than its German counterpart to discourage frivolous and underserving litigation.[13]

If, in accordance with the above, a *definitive* economic justification for the different solutions of foreign law remains elusive, the same is not true when we move to the wider philosophical reasons which lie at the root of these (foreign) liability rules. As already stated, we find both French and German law in broad agreement as to (a) the need to control statutory bodies, (b) their willingness to do this by using all possible means at their disposal including the courts, and (c) their complete contempt for the argument that such control would make the civil servants in question reluctant to act. All of us have much sympathy with these positions of principle; and we do not regard them as being fundamentally alien to the common law frame of mind. To support this assertion we rely on sections of Lord Reid's judgments given in the *Dorset Yacht*[14] case; Lord Bingham's most recent judicial work and, more precisely, his *dicta* in the *X* v. *Bedfordshire* case;[15] and, to some extent, Lord Hutton's strongly voiced doubts in *Barrett* about the validity of some of the arguments that led to the defeat of the plaintiff's action in *X* v. *Bedfordshire.* We thus feel considerable sympathy for the argument that it may be unfair to place, almost as a matter of course, the burden of administration activities carried out for the com-

---

[13] Which is Lord Browne Wilkinson's main worry. See his comments in his speech to the Education Law Association, cited above at n. 5.

[14] [1970] 2 WLR 1140, 1145 *ff.*

[15] In particular the tenor of his argument in his judgment in the Court of Appeal in the *Newham* and *Bedfordshire* cases [1994] 2 WLR 554.

mon weal on any individual person. On this count, therefore, we are inclined to think that the current English solutions – not, it must be stressed again, shared by all of our senior serving judges[16] – have been dictated by excessive caution and unconfirmed economic intuitions, rather than by any evidence, empirical or comparative, which makes such solutions incontrovertible.

Let us then move further from methodology and philosophy to substantive law. Before we proceed to make more concrete observations on the current state of English law, we feel that it is necessary to stress the importance of the foreign material we have used in this book. Irrespective of whether or not the reader finds it convincing the fact is that, on the whole, the views given above on French and German law reflect the state of thinking found in most of Europe. This means that this material is not only interesting in itself, but also goes a long way towards explaining the underlying suspicions the Strasbourg Court may have felt of the English judgments which, *de facto* if not *de iure*,[17] have, over the years, established wide-ranging immunities for a wide range of statutory bodies. Seen in this context, what is of interest to us is not that the Strasbourg Court took the view it did in the *Osman* case, but that this view received the support of even the English judge. Thus, those who agree with Lord Hoffmann and who accuse the Strasbourg Court of not having understood how English law works, might wish to consider the possibility that their own preoccupation with "efficient allocation of scarce resources" may have led them to underestimate

[16] Thus, see, for example, Lord Nicholls' eloquent dissenting judgment in *Stovin* v. *Wise* [1996] 3 WLR 388, 392 *ff.*, especially 402 *ff.* where he departs from Lord Hoffmann's approach in many significant respects.

[17] Before the Strasbourg Court government lawyers attempted to emphasise a number of cases which showed that the immunity conferred on the police was not, in fact, a blanket immunity. However, of the five cases which they cited imposing liability on the police, only one – *Swinney* – is post-*Hill*. Thus, although these decisions may still stand on their facts, they do not seem to reflect the new trend in favour of immunity which was, if anything, reinforced by the cases considered in this book, especially the *Bedfordshire*, *Stovin* and *Elguzouli* decisions.

the wider political, legal and moral considerations that weigh so heavily in the minds of many leading European jurists. To imply that their views do not really matter any longer now that we have brought human rights "back home" is, with the greatest respect, totally unconvincing. For, not only does it ignore the continued influence that Strasbourg jurisprudence will have (even after the Human Rights Act 1998 comes into force), but also because it underestimates the wider infiltration of European thinking currently taking place in this country and evidenced by the plethora of judicial and extra-judicial pronouncements of some of our most academically minded judges. Just as important is our conviction that if our understanding of the European position is accurate – at least in its philosophical undertones – we must be right in our assertion that Strasbourg will continue to abide by the position it adopted in *Osman*. This, too, is an important point since it suggests that English judges may be disappointed if they try to "wish" *Osman* away.[18]

Secondly, we wish to stress that our criticism of English law is based on a combination of comparative material and economic analysis. With regard to the latter, the starting point may well be that this kind of (economic) reasoning may best be suited to specialist academics. This is not to say, however, that the judges are wrong to consider the wider economic implica-

---

[18] We put forward this idea tentatively and in the light of two facts: first, we note that apart from Lord Browne-Wilkinson, the two judges who gave leading judgments in *Barrett* were able to dispose of the case without any reference to *Osman*. Secondly, we recall how the House of Lords – unlike the Court of Appeal – tried in *Derbyshire County Council* v. *Times* [1993] AC 534 to argue – unconvincingly in our view – that the result reached in that case owed nothing to the background influence of the European Convention on Human Rights. We, therefore, respectively agree with Lord Justice Pill when, in his judgment in *Palmer* v. *Tees Health Authority* (1999) *The Times*, 6 July he referred to *Osman* as a decision that "weighed heavily upon the decision in *Barrett*" in the House of Lords. (The quotation comes from the transcript of the, as yet, unreported decision.) The *Osman* influence can also be detected in *Brindle* v. *Commissioner of Police for the Metropolis*, 29 March 1999 (un-reported at the time of writing) and *Swinney* v. *Chief Constable of Northumbria Police* (No. 2), *The Times*, 25 May 1999.

tions of the imposition of liability upon public bodies or to try to add this weapon to their armoury. On the contrary, we feel that Lord Hoffmann's attempt in *Stovin* v. *Wise* to introduce a degree of rigour and clarity to the economic debate is to be welcomed and encouraged. However, Lord Hoffmann's formulation of the economic issues should – we hope – be seen as a most commendable effort to spark off a debate but, most assuredly, not as having concluded it. What is at issue here is not simply the conclusions he reached on the substance of the economic case (which we have considered above), but also his overall approach to the use of economics in cases of this kind. From this latter perspective, Lord Hoffmann's approach can be questioned for the excessive certainty with which predictions of the effects of liability rules were put forward. As we explained in Chapter One, "positive" or predictive economic analysis should properly involve two stages, and the formulation of predictions or hypotheses using axiomatic economic reasoning is only the first of these. The second stage involves the testing of hypotheses using empirical research techniques. The fact that this is expensive and is rarely done (even by many law and economics scholars) is no reason to believe that it is not important. At the risk of repeating ourselves, this is not to suggest that the courts should completely eschew economic reasoning on the grounds that they lack the resources to test economic propositions in this way. However, we do suggest that the courts should treat economic predictions of the impact of liability rules with appropriate caution. In due course, it may be possible for the courts and counsel to develop procedures whereby the relevant economic literature on a given question is properly canvassed and assessed (as already happens in the context of competition policy cases and some others). Until that is done, however, care is needed in the way economic evidence is used.

A further and wider observation relates to the relationship between economic and non-economic values. As we showed in Chapter One, it is essential to clarify what is meant by "economic efficiency" in this context. The criteria by which efficiency is judged – mainly, in the context of tort law, allocative efficiency – provide us with useful means for assessing whether particular outcomes are more or less likely to enhance the wealth or well-being of society. Even if they can be successfully deployed to this end, they do not tell us how to weigh economic efficiency against other values. Above all, they tell us nothing about how individual rights are to be weighed against efficiency in the case of conflicts between them. Economics can help to clarify the issues when such conflicts occur, so that we get a clearer picture of the nature and extent of the trade-offs which may be involved, but what it cannot do is provide us with an infallible calculus for resolving these trade-offs. In the final analysis, that involves judgments which lie beyond economics. The recent obsession of the courts with "budgetary issues" and "efficient government" to the exclusion of other values – a point which becomes particularly obvious when we compare contemporary English law with French and German – has not only prevented its advocates from exploring the possible deterrent value of holding the police and other statutory bodies liable for their negligent actions, it also means that the courts have failed to appreciate the significance of the not inconsiderable philosophical point, so dear to most European legal systems, that the courts are there precisely to effect this extra kind of control and keep the administration, in all its emanations, in check.

A substantial part of this book has also been devoted to making a number of more specific assertions above the current state of English law, some of which, we suspect, are more acceptable than others. The most incontrovertible assertion is that our courts have, in the space of the last ten years or so, shifted their justification process from a legal or legalistic one, to one which is distinctly more policy-oriented. We predict that this will have both welcome and unexplored consequences.

The reorientation will be welcome because it will make us all address real issues and concerns rather than use legal concepts in an excessively formalistic way to conceal the true basis for the court's reasoning (where the comparison with other systems may become relevant and even, give English law, the edge, if it makes proper use of this extra-legal material). But this approach also has consequences which, if we are honest about this matter, have yet properly to be fathomed.

Thus, how will practitioners henceforth proceed to distinguish their case from earlier ones when the argumentation brought into fashion by cases such as *X* v. *Bedfordshire* and the majority judgment in *Stovin* are so obviously different – in content and style – from the one that has prevailed for centuries? We can imagine at least three possible tendencies emerging from this current, unsatisfactory[19] state of affairs.

First, some judges will, no doubt, take their cue from the judgments of Lords Slynn and Hutton in *Barrett* and attempt to show that, what for brevity's sake we call the Browne-Wilkinson policy arguments in *X* v. *Bedfordshire* are inapplicable to the case before them. The merits of such tactics will be that they will avoid (or rather postpone) an *open* confrontation with Strasbourg. Such tactics may also offer barristers a sense of (false) security in that will make them feel that they are back on familiar turf arguing and distinguishing cases on the basis of ingenious distinctions and not banding about general and often un-provable policy assertions. The demerits of such an approach may, however, be even greater than the perceived advantages. For this way of proceeding will, undoubtedly, contribute to the increase in litigation, which – we must always remember – our judges fear most than anything else. More importantly, it will fail to address the core argument of the current orthodoxy. This is the theory of "economic efficiency" as enunciated most clearly by Lord Hoffmann but also consistently present in the judgments of those who have adopted his philosophy. Such a way of dealing with *Osman* will thus, in our view, be based on distinctions that will often cross the line that divides

---

[19] We call the current situation unsatisfactory not only because we are, ourselves, unhappy with the five cases we have discussed in this book but also because we detect considerable judicial uncertainty as to how *Osman* should be handled. This, apart from *Barrett*, see *Palmer* v. *Tees Health Authority*, 2 June 1999 and *David Gower* v. *London Borough of Bromley*, 29 July 1999 – both unreported at the time of going to the press.

the ingenious from the ingenuous and thus will not be conducive to a principled development of the law.[20]

A second approach has been indicated by the recent decision of the Court of Appeal in *Palmer* v. *Tees Health Authority*.[21] What we see, here, especially in the two majority judgments, is an attempt to retain the "striking out" mechanism by saying that *Osman* only prohibited it through the use of the device of "fair, just and reasonable". Some admittedly vague pronouncements on this point in *Osman* thus allowed the majority in *Palmer* to argue that "striking out" was still possible on grounds of "lack of proximity". Those who like us believe that, foreseeability, proximity and "fair just and reasonable" all-too-easily slide into one another – and it would appear that Lord Justice Pill in *Palmer* is one of them – will find this way of "evading" *Osman* entirely unconvincing. For in our view, it runs so counter to Strasbourg's main philosophy as expressed overall in that judgment that any attempt to side-step Strasbourg in such a manner will be a new invitation to that court to intervene in our law. Once again, therefore, we see this as a half-backed response to clear signals from abroad that a real change is needed in our practices if further reversals by Strasbourg are to be avoided.

So this brings us to the third and most profitable way of proceeding. In our view this consists in first and foremost appreciating the reasons why Strasbourg reached the conclusion it did, rather than accusing its judges of not understanding our "strike out" procedures. This, as stated in this book, involves understanding the wider practice that prevails in Europe and which must surely be seen as "normal" by most of the Strasbourg judges. Secondly, it means weighing the kind of comparative and economic arguments we have presented in this paper and accepting that the basic economic philosophy that underlies our

[20] Which some of our judges nowadays seem to think is highly desirable. See, for instance, Lord Mustill in his dissenting judgment in *White* v. *Jones* [1995] 2 WLR 187, 228E and Lord Hoffmann in *Hunter* v. *Canary Wharf Ltd* [1997] 2 WLR 684, 709F.

[21] *The Times*, 6 July 1999. Our comments are based on the as yet unpublished full transcript of the judgments.

current (*ante Barrett*) judicial thought is at best not fully worked out and at worst flawed. Thirdly, it means devising a way for "keeping matters under control" that is workable in practice and methodologically acceptable to our judges. This must surely be by shifting their emphasis from "duty" to "careless breach" and "causation" and, in the end, rejecting unmeritorious claim on those grounds rather than through summary decisions on the basis of assumed facts. The fact that events are assumed to be as the plaintiff alleges them to be is of little use to him. For, as we have noted time and again, in practice if not in theory, the response of the courts has been almost constantly to hold that there is "no duty" and thus no right to be tested and, if proved, enforced by them. Of course, friends of the *ante Barrett* status quo will be quick to point out that this way of proceeding may lead to an increase in litigation. We accept this as a risk but not as one that is greater than the increase of litigation that will be provoked by the *Palmer* or *Barrett* type of reasoning that we sketched above. Moreover, if such an increase in litigation does occur, we believe it could be short-lived. For, first, we are constantly reminded these days of how legal aid makes it increasingly difficult to resort to litigation. Secondly, we also feel confident that the first cluster of cases, if decided on the basis of clear and rational criteria (and not the ones that we rejected in the previous paragraphs), should be able to send clear signals to litigants as to which claims should be settled and which resisted. Thus, we suspect, few will doubt that the "careless breach" requirement is easily justified in, say, the *Essex* case; but not easily satisfied in cases such as *Bedfordshire* and *Barrett*. The assumptions we are putting forward will, in most disputes, be shared by Counsel who must realise (as law students do not) that the current victories won against the "strike out actions" approach, do not, necessarily, mean final victory for the plaintiffs. Proceeding with litigation will thus still remain the last resort, not to be undertaken lightly.

Secondly, we have suggested that in the material reviewed in this book our courts have moved slowly but steadily much further than the *Hill* facts (and judgments) originally called for.

The almost complete shift from legal concepts to policy has made possible such a change in results. The multiplication of "affective immunities" has thus spread to cover not only the police but also welfare authorities, educational authorities, the public prosecution service and other emergency services in a way that in its amplitude has no real counterparts either in the Continent of Europe or, even, the USA. Yet the legal outcome in some of the most recent decisions may be seen by many as an affront – in some cases a serious affront – to basic notions of justice. In short, paraphrasing Lord Justice Ward,[22] the pursuit of the greater public good at the expense of individual hardship can go so far and no further. If that is, indeed, the view which continues to prevail, these results will not prove long-lived. Justice – unquantifiable, immeasurable and vague though it may be – remains an important aim of the law in general, and of the law of torts in particular. The advocates of financial prudence and efficiency cannot use this virtue, however desirable it is, to trump so many well-established aims of tort law such as compensation, justice, deterrence,[23] and even retribution. A more measured result must be achieved and, so far, all of us feel that this has eluded English law. Our reading of the Strasbourg decision(s) encourages us in the belief that this European influence will, along with others mentioned in this book, force the English courts to re-examine and, we hope, redefine (in an as yet unpredictable way) some of their absolute immunity rules.

Finally, we have described briefly two foreign legal systems. Although their structures and concepts are, as we have freely admitted, different to ours, the systems operate in political, social and economic environments, which are *broadly* similar (although with cyclical variations of emphasis from centre/right to centre/left and back again). The way these problems are handled in the judicial decisions (of Germany and, more so, France)

[22] *Swinney* v. *Chief Constable of Northumbria Police Force* [1997] QB 464, 487.

[23] We thus agree with Lord Justice Bingham (as he then was) when, in the Court of Appeal in *X* v. *Bedfordshire* [1994] 2 WLR 554, 662G he said, "I cannot accept, as a general proposition, that the imposition of a duty of care makes no contribution to the maintenance of high standards".

may make some English lawyers feel proud of their judicial techniques and reasoning process. We think there is some truth in such an assertion. Equally, we feel that foreign judges might learn from studying the form and style of common law judgments. However, the foreign solutions (if not the judgments themselves) also suggest that the fears and arguments advanced in England to stunt the imposition of civil liability have not materialised abroad. Such a stark contrast, especially in what is the proper ambit of state responsibility, merits at the very least a more detailed study than we have managed to carry out so far in order to determine who is right: our neighbours or us. Such study will yield the incidental benefit of telling us something about our style of reasoning[24] and of our legal concepts – their weak and strong points – and their ability to survive in the future. More importantly, it will encourage our lawyers – students and practitioners alike – to keep the European dimension constantly in front of their eyes. The *Osman* decision suggests that Europe – love it or hate it – and its ideas will continue to be a source of controversy, irritation and, as far as we are concerned, inspiration for many years to come.

---

[24] Some authors have already carried out research which shows that, for instance, the French and English reasoning processes are more similar than they appear to be at first sight. Thus, see, J Bell, "Reflections on the Procedure of the Conseil d' Etat" in G Hand and J McBride (eds), *Droit sans Frontiers* (1991), 211 *ff*. The value of this research and their conclusions are beyond dispute; but our examination of these cases also shows that, in this type of situation, the reasoning process and style are quite different. This can only confirm the widely held view that in comparative studies the warning against generalisations must be made constantly!

Appendices
A Brief Note to the Seven Cases That Follow

The first seven cases reproduced in translated form were selected from a number of German decisions which dealt with the issues raised in the five English cases which were the subject of the present discussion. As our notes to the preceding text show, other decisions exist to prove that, in its broad outline, the case law has remained constant and without adverse effects to the system as a whole. What, however, our readers will not encounter in the preceding pages is a comparison between the styles and forms of the judgments of the two countries. This is partly because the first of us has already penned some thoughts on this subject elsewhere;[1] but also because he hopes to return to the same topic in a forthcoming *Festschrift* honouring a distinguished German colleague: Professor Peter Schlechtriem. The deliberate omission of comparative comments on differing styles should not, however, be taken as a sign of lesser importance. "Style", as Edward Gibbon (himself a great stylist) once observed, "is the image of character".[2] We can thus learn much about how people in general, and judges in particular, think by studying the way in which they choose to express themselves in their texts. More important, however, is the arguable point that even if one disagrees with the results reached by the English courts, one cannot help admiring the style of their judgments and the multiplicity of arguments are increasingly willing to marshal when trying to reach the right result. Thus, some of us

[1] B S Markesinis, "A Matter of Style" (1994) 110 *Law Quarterly Review*, 607–8.
[2] *Memoirs of My Life*, B Radice (ed.) (1991), 39.

at least would be happy if, as a result of our efforts, the English considered more the philosophical stance which lies at the basis of the foreign solutions, and the French and Germans explored the possibility of using a wider variety of tools than they openly do at present .

Two more points deserve to be made: one narrow and the other wider. The narrow point is related to the extensive use which German lawyers make of the so-called *Normzwecktheorie*. Despite its name, there is nothing alien in this approach since it is also widely used by common lawyers when deciding, for instance, whether breach of a statutory duty gives rise to a civil remedy for the benefit of an individual plaintiff.

The wider point comes out most clearly when we look at the last two translations included in this batch which deal with the troublesome problem of damage caused *to* the product and not damage caused *by* the product in the context of factual disputes which come very close to *Dutton* v. *Bognor Regis Urban District Council*[3] and *Anns* v. *Merton London Borough*.[4] The German cases, it will be noticed, correctly characterised the plaintiffs' loss as pure economic loss. By contrast, English law originally chose to call this loss material damage to property. Although these German decisions were – through counsel – submitted to the House of Lords, they were ignored. Thus, it was not until 1985 that the House of Lords saw the errors of its ways on this particular point. See *Peabody Donation Fund* v. *Sir Lindsay Parkinson and Co. Ltd.*[5] A greater willingness to look at foreign law might well have saved much indigenous effort. Thus, for comparative lawyers, it must be an important part of their work to bring to the attention of national lawyers the opportunity of taking advantage of foreign ideas. It must also, surely, be the duty of every broad-minded jurist to consider at least the possibility that he or she might stand to learn from the intellectual toils of his foreign colleagues. Lack of time is a poor reason for not even making the effort.

[3] [1972] 1 QB 373.
[4] [1978] AC 728.
[5] [1985] AC 210.

BGH LM § 839 [Fg] BGB No. 5, judgment of 30 April 1953 – III ZR 204/52 (Hamm)[1]

Reasons

The defendant asks first for a re-examination of the appeal court's opinion that the police officers were under an official duty to take action against the members of a gang of thieves, two of whom later committed a break-in at the plaintiff's residence. The appeal in law refers in this connection to the decision of 11 June 1952 [reference omitted]. There is no ground to deviate from the principles set out in this decision. Accordingly, it cannot be doubted that the police officers were under a duty to take action against those members of the gang who were known to them and who were committing crimes in their area of operation. According to the indisputable facts of the case, it was known to H [one of the police officers] that, among other things, N, who took part in the later break-in at the plaintiff's residence had committed a burglary with two other people. However, in his examination as a witness in the main proceedings before the *Schöffengericht* (lay assessors court) because of this theft, he deliberately gave false evidence in order to help N, who was in fact acquitted, as were the other perpetrators, for lack of evidence. Shortly afterwards, K as well as H found out the names of all those involved in the burglary. Both, however, still failed to bring a criminal charge. H and K therefore had definite knowledge of the serious crimes committed by the gang and in particular of the co-perpetrators of the break-in later committed at the plaintiff's. This left them no room for discretion when deciding whether measures were necessary against the perpetrators known to them. Criminal prosecution of law-breakers and preventing crimes came within the scope of the official tasks of the two officers as police officers. Non-intervention by them in the given situation could not be justified by any sort of objective or policing considerations. Remaining inactive was unambiguously outside the boundary of discretion of "harmfulness". A

[1] Translated by Mr Raymond Youngs, Southampton Institute.

situation of danger was present which made action by the police officers an unconditional duty.

1. The question was raised in the said decision of how the establishment of the boundaries of discretion of "harmfulness" or of "excess" is to be treated in the individual case. Was it a pure issue of law and to be undertaken by the court "in accordance with relevant considerations" [reference omitted]? Or was it a question here of a "pure issue of discretion" to be decided by the appropriate authority, which the judge cannot generally re-examine [reference omitted]? No final position needs to be taken here on this question. Even if the establishment of the boundaries of discretion is in principle regarded as a "pure issue of discretion" which cannot generally be re-examined judicially, the police officers involved were still under a duty to take action. This is because we have a case here in which even a decision based on discretion (which is not in principle subject to judicial re-examination) can still be subjected to such a re-examination. The officers' failure to act was not based on a weighing-up of the arguments for and against in accordance with objective considerations, but was based exclusively on irrelevant and purely personal grounds. They therefore have acted with such a high degree of impropriety that their behaviour – and this needs no further explanation in the given circumstances – is irreconcilable with the requirements of proper police administration and does not satisfy the needs of proper administration from any possible point of view [references omitted].

2. The further question of whether the official duty violated by the police officers by failing to act against the gang also existed against the plaintiff as a "third party" in the sense of § 839 of the BGB was, likewise, correctly answered in the affirmative by the appeal court.

According to the case law of the *Reichsgericht* [reference omitted], which the Senate followed in [reference omitted], the question of whether an official duty is owed by an official to a third party is to be adjudged taking into consideration the officer's official area of activity and the type of work which he is carrying out. In this connection the main emphasis is on the purpose which the official duty is to serve. If this is imposed on the officer in the interests of individual persons, everyone whose interests are, according to the special nature of the official business, affected by it will be a third party. But if the purpose of the official duty is only the maintenance of public order or the interest which the state has in officials carrying out the responsibilities of their office properly, the official owes no duty to third parties, even if there is indirect intrusion into the interests of third parties by the exercise of this duty. The task of preventing crimes is not however owed by the police in the interest of the general public alone, but, as to crimes which also intrude directly into the protected legal sphere of the individual, to the endangered individuals as well. If the police do not properly fulfil this task, this not only violates a duty owed by the police to the general public but also a duty owed by it to the endangered individuals.

The appeal in law refers in this connection to the decision of the *Reichsgericht* in [reference omitted] in which the duty imposed on the state prosecutor by § 152(2) of the Criminal Procedure Code to prosecute for crimes is described as a task serving exclusively the interests of the general public. It then takes the view that in this respect the task of the *police* could not be regarded in any different way. But it can be left open in this case whether and, if appropriate, how the area of responsibility of the state prosecutor and of the police is to be judged differently in relation to the prosecution of crimes. This is because the issue is not the duty of criminal prosecution incumbent on both authorities but the duty to prevent crimes, which falls on the police as a task arising directly from their duty of protection from danger. For the state prosecutor a general direct responsibility to prevent crimes does not exist; at the most it arises only insofar as the purpose of prosecution for crime is to prevent further crime. In this respect therefore the reference to the decision of the *Reichsgericht* mentioned above misses the point.

The appeal in law further takes the view, having regard to [references omitted], that the general duty of protection by the police (and therefore also their duty to prevent crimes) is not a duty owed to third parties but only to the general public. This would be so at least as long as no concrete relationship to a definite third party has yet developed and the actual person harmed has not so far stood out from the mass of people who could be harmed. In the present case, no such actual relationship to a particular person harmed has yet been established. The possible crimes which lawbreakers known to police officers might commit could have been directed against simply any inhabitant of the area concerned and therefore against an entirely undetermined circle of people. The duty of the officers was owed only to the general public and not the plaintiff as a member of the general public, which should be protected. That cannot however be agreed. A person who stands out from the mass of people at risk because he was specially at risk is not the only person to be regarded as a third party to whom the police owe a duty to prevent crimes, as was the case with the facts which formed the basis of the decision [reference omitted]. The circle of third parties should be drawn much more widely. Thus the *Reichsgericht* has, among other things, regarded the fulfilment of the general protective duty of care (subject to the prerequisite that exercise of public power is in question) as among the official duties owed by an official to every third party [reference omitted] and confirmed that the official duty of a teacher supervising a ball game is owed to anyone not participating who could come into the area of the game [reference omitted]. Accordingly, the duty of an official to prevent improper use of service vehicles has also been described by the Senate in the decision [reference omitted] as an official duty which exists against every highway user with whom the vehicle could come in contact while it is being improperly used. Therefore the duty of the police to prevent crimes must also be regarded as an official duty which is owed to anyone whose legal interests are endangered by a violation of this duty.

In the present case the following additional considerations also arise in this connection. All officials entrusted with the exercise of public power have an official duty to refrain from any misuse of their office. An official can make himself guilty of an improper exercise of office by omitting to act within the framework of the public power entrusted to him. That is always the case when the official duty unambiguously requires such action but the action does not take place because of completely irrelevant, purely personal and reprehensible reasons. It needs no further discussion that the police officers H and K have made themselves guilty in this respect of a misuse of office. However, the duty to refrain from any misuse of office is owed by the officials to anyone who could be harmed by the misuse [references omitted]. It cannot therefore be doubted that the official duty of the police officers to act as police against the gang was also owed to the plaintiff.

BGH NJW 1980, 2194, BGH judgment of 10 July 1980 – III ZR 58/79 (Braunschweig)[2]

Facts

The plaintiff demands compensation from the defendant city because of violation of the duty of protective care in relation to highways. On 3 June 1975 at about 9.45 pm the plaintiff's wife, who was driving the plaintiff's car, turned left at a dual carriageway (the A Ring). There was a hedge (which has since been removed) approximately 1.2 metres in height on the central reservation. The plaintiff's wife crossed the lane which led to her right, drove through a gap in the central reservation, tried to turn into the lane leading left and collided with a car approaching from the left. The plaintiff claimed that his wife edged carefully into the lane and could not see the other vehicle in time because the hedge was too high.

Grounds

I. The appeal court found no violation of the defendant's duty of protective care and in this connection stated that the central reservation did not form part of the highway. It was true that a duty to warn about limitations on visibility, which were not obvious (or to remove them), could also exist for areas outside the

---

[2] Translated by Mr Raymond Youngs, Southampton Institute.

street. But here the restriction on visibility caused by the hedge was obvious anyway. The danger was in the end due to the conduct of the plaintiff's wife, who turned to the left without taking sufficient precautions. A reasonably experienced driver would have been able to cope with the situation in question. Besides this, a claim under § 839(1), sentence 2 of the BGB would not arise as the plaintiff has another option for compensation by claiming against his wife.

There are fundamental legal objections to this judgment.

II. 1. The appeal court's starting point, that a violation of the duty of protective care in relation to highways by the officers of the defendant is to be assessed in accordance with the provisions on official liability (§ 839 of the BGB, Article 34 of the GG), is certainly correct. According to § 10, paragraph 1 of the Highways Act of Lower Saxony of 14 December 1962 [reference omitted] the building and maintenance of public highways (inclusive of the federal trunk roads) and surveillance of their safety for traffic falls on the organs and public employees of the body dealing with them, as an official duty in exercise of state activity. This formulation contained in the public law statutes of the state *(Land)* of the duties of the office holder of a municipality *(Gemeinde)* in ensuring traffic safety on public highways is – as the Senate has explained in the judgments [references omitted] – permissible in the context of the division of legislative competence between the Federation and the states. Nor are there any other constitutional law objections to it derived from the Basic Law.

2. The Senate's judgment [reference omitted] explains in detail that a body liable for breach of official duty cannot rely on the provisions of § 839(1), sentence 2 of the BGB as they contradict the basic principle of the equal treatment of highway users in liability law. These principles also apply, as the Senate has explained in more detail in the judgment [reference omitted] (issued after the publication of the judgment in the appeal) for cases like this one involving surveillance of traffic safety on a public highway, if this duty falls on the office holder as a state

responsibility. The official duty to ensure safety of road traffic is closely related to the duties owed by an official as a public highway user. Accordingly the defendant city cannot exonerate itself by reference to the possibility that the plaintiff's wife is liable for the accident.

3. The appeal court's finding that there was no violation of the duty of protective care in relation to highways cannot be endorsed either.

(a) The official duty formulated in public law to ensure the safety of road traffic corresponds in its content to the general duty of protective care [references omitted]. Its scope is determined by the type and frequency of use of the highway and its importance. It includes the necessary measures for the creation and maintenance of road conditions, which are sufficiently safe for road users. It is true that a road user must in principle adjust to the given road conditions and accept the highway in the form in which it appears to him. A party under a duty of protective care must, in an appropriate and objectively reasonable manner, remove (and if necessary warn about) all those dangers (but no others) which are not visible or not visible in time for a highway user who is exercising the necessary care and to which he cannot adjust or cannot adjust in time.

(b) In applying these principles to the present case, an official duty by the public employees of the defendant must be accepted to keep the hedge at a height which prevents serious obstruction of visibility for road users on turning into the highway from an access. The appeal court interprets the concept of the highway too narrowly when it includes in it, apart from the carriageway, only those surfaces which "also serve traffic in some way or other e.g. for escape in case of emergency. . .". According to both § 2II, No. 1 Lower Saxony Highways Act and §1IV, No. 1 Federal Highways Act in the 1 October 1974 version [reference omitted] separation strips, verges, and marginal and safety strips are also included in public highways [references omitted]. As federal and state law agree here, it has no significance for the outcome of the case whether the A Ring was a federal, state or municipality highway. According to these statutory rules, the duty of protective care extends to the central reservation as a part of the highway. It is therefore not necessary to fall back on the case law cited by the appeal court according to which the duty of protective care extends to things not forming part of the highway insofar as they represent a danger for the use of the highway, as for instance trees and shrubs in front gardens [references omitted]. Nor is it necessary to refer to the duties, which fall on the owner of the hedge as such.

(c) A high hedge created special dangers in a place where there was a gap in the central reservation to enable highway users to turn in and out of it. Drivers turning in could only be sure of seeing the traffic on the other side of the hedge if the hedge was at least, for an appropriate distance from the entrance, kept low enough for it not significantly to conceal moving vehicles behind it. Contrary to the view of the appeal court, this danger did not cease in whole or in part to arise just because the hedge could be seen, and because this was so even in darkness, with the help of street lighting and car headlights. The danger was not the hedge itself, but the hindrance to visibility, which it caused, and this hindrance did not cease to exist just because the hedge was visible.

(d) The defendant city claimed in its submissions that it complied with these principles. According to these submissions, hedges are cut once-yearly, and twice-yearly at traffic focal points, and kept in "shape". The end sections of a hedge before and after accesses are cut back further than the middle parts of the hedge. Actually, however, the defendant has not kept to these principles in the area of the site of the accident, according to the findings of the appeal court. The shrubs situated on the central reservation had reached a height of about 1.2 metres on the day of the accident. The appeal court has described the hindrance to visibility consequently occurring as "obvious" and in another place has spoken of a hedge height "undoubtedly hindering visibility". But it regarded this as insignificant for the outcome of the case, because every driver could escape the threat of danger which this caused, either by increased attention on turning in or out or by the choice of another driving route. This view is, it should be acknowledged in support of the appeal in law, affected by legal error.

(aa) A driver must certainly in principle accept the highway as it presents itself to him, and therefore make his own investigations as to whether he has sufficient visibility. The hedge height of about 1.2 metres could however seriously hinder the necessary visibility even for an attentive driver, and the appeal court has not paid sufficient attention to this. According to the findings of the *Landgericht*, the height of vision of the plaintiff's wife in his car used in the accident . . . was 1.1 metres, and that of an assessor of the *Landgericht* 1.2 metres. Cars of the usual construction, as is revealed by type surveys in the press, are without exception between 1.3 and 1.5 metres high. Cars of this type protruded, at the most, only marginally above the hedge. The extent to which they were visible depended to a large degree on their type of construction. The defendant city could in any case not act on the basis that drivers would, on turning at the site of the accident, see cars approaching behind the hedge in time in every case. This possible danger which, as the appeal court has pertinently explained, could not be removed by a warning sign, resulted in the hindrance to visibility caused by the 1.2 metre-high hedge at the site of the accident being dangerous even for an attentive driver. A careful tentative entry – which the appeal court did not even consider to be necessary – into the lane situated on the other side of the hedge could not remove these dangers. This is because a sufficient view could not be obtained of this lane *before* turning into it. That follows from the finding of the appeal court about the effect which the hedge had in restricting visibility.

(bb) The duty of ensuring traffic safety did not cease to apply, as the appeal court thought it did, just because no driver *had* to turn in at the place in question. It cannot in principle be held against highway users by a party under a duty of protective care that they should have avoided dangerous places. This would enable the party to shift its responsibility to the driver in an impermissible manner. It is the task of the party under the duty of protective care either to remove or at least to defuse danger spots which it can recognise as such so far as is reasonable and as soon as possible.

(cc) The party under the duty of protective care must further protect traffic from the mistakes which, according to experience, are exactly what has to be reckoned with in heavy traffic in large cities – here, underestimating the dangers caused by restriction of visibility and possible violations of the right of way. The principle of trust, which applies to the mutual relationship of highway users, has no application in the relationship between the party under a duty of protective care and highway users. On the contrary, the duty of protective care can include in individual cases those measures which have the purpose of protecting traffic from the consequences of inappropriate conduct of individual highway users [reference omitted].

These prerequisites are present here. In the heavy traffic in inner cities, violations of rules of priority are not rare. If visibility of the road having priority is substantially impaired, and a particularly careful driving style is indicated (taking up more time than usual), one must reckon on more frequent violations of these duties. The defendant city could also have recognised this. Regular cutting of the hedge down to 70–80 centimetres in height was therefore obviously required. This relatively simple and cheap measure was to be expected of the defendant – and pertinently the appeal court accepted this.

4. The disputed judgment also cannot be based on different reasoning. It is not possible to proceed on the basis that the violation by the defendant city of the duty of protective care is completely superseded by the contribution of the plaintiff's wife to the accident. According to her statement as witness, the plaintiff's wife – in contrast to the case decided by the Kammergericht which was otherwise similar [reference omitted] – did not turn into the space behind the hedge without any regard to the restriction on visibility. Instead, she claims at first to have stopped briefly and only after starting off again to have collided with the other car, which had approached in the meantime. It may be that, as a result of carelessness, she did not pay attention or sufficient attention to the distance and speed of this vehi-

cle, because it approached on the left lane of the carriageway (its driver wanting to turn to the left further on). Nevertheless, it cannot be assumed that there would have been a collision even without the restriction of visibility by the hedge, especially as it has to be borne in mind that the driver of the other car was also unable to see, in sufficient time, the car driven by the plaintiff's wife turning in because of the hedge.

5. The matter must be referred back to the appeal court, because the weighing-up in accordance with § 254 of the BGB of the extent of the contributions to the accident from both sides is not possible according to the findings which have been made, and must remain an issue for the judge of fact.

BGH NJW 1996, 2373, BGH Decision of 28 March 1996 – III ZR 141/95 (Düsseldorf)[3]

Facts

The A Group offered facilities for investment of capital for small investors. In October 1987, because of a fall in share prices, the group suffered heavy losses so that the whole capital investment was exhausted. This was concealed from the investors, and the group carried on advertising investment facilities. The state prosecutor took investigatory proceedings against those responsible. The group's money deposited with a bank was first of all seized, but the Amtsgericht (district court) quashed the seizure and the state prosecutor discontinued the investigatory proceedings. Five months later, the plaintiff made a financial management contract with the A Group. Over a year later the A Group suffered further heavy losses and the investigatory proceedings were recommenced against those responsible which led to their conviction for deceit. The plaintiff, who had lost about three-quarters of his capital, claimed compensation from the defendant state (Land).

Grounds

The case is not of significance on an issue of principle; and the appeal in law has no prospect of success [reference omitted].

1. The appeal court denied that the official duty of the state prosecutor to pursue crimes, to carry out investigatory proceedings against the perpetrators and, if necessary, to start a public prosecution is owed to third parties. It stated that this duty was exclusively to serve public interests, namely the fulfilment of the criminal powers of the state. The arguments raised in the appeal in law against this are unsuccessful. The introduction of investigatory proceedings in criminal law, the initiation and execution of a search order, a decision about the starting of a public prosecution and measures in proceedings for fines can represent violations of the official duty owed to the suspect if they are undertaken without justification [references omitted]. But there is no official duty on the part of the state prosecutor to intervene in the interest of a person possibly affected by a crime – in contrast to the position in relation to the police (see *Senate*, LM § 839 [Fg] BGB No. 5). The duty of the state prosecutor to pursue crimes, to arrest an accused, etc., exists only in the public interest. Failure to carry it out cannot therefore, as a rule, violate an official duty against the person harmed by the crime [references omitted]. It can be otherwise if concrete protective duties to the person harmed by a crime are acquired by the state prosecutor in current investigatory proceedings, perhaps to secure stolen property in the interests of the person from whom it has been stolen [references omitted]. The principles set out above also apply to the prevention of crimes, which is the issue in the case of plaintiff.

2. As the appeal court further states, the plaintiff did not, in May 1988, come within the category of those who had already paid their money to the A Group. They could not therefore possibly have been protected from harm by the seizure being kept in force and the proceedings against the suspects being pursued on the grounds that those steps would have deprived the suspects of access to further accounts. As the plaintiff first made his investment on 18 June 1988, he was not directly affected by the decision of the state prosecutor to order the quashing of the seizure and to discontinue the proceedings on 2 May 1988 [reference omitted]. The harm he has suffered is based on the fact

that the accused persons had not been forced to give up their activity. It can however be left undecided whether, if an official duty on the part of the state prosecutor owed to third parties suffering harm could be accepted, this would stand in the way of including the plaintiff within the circle of those protected (see *Senate*, LM § 839 [Fg] BGB No. 5), as the duty is not owed to third parties.

3. The appeal court judgment does not reveal any other legal errors, which are significant in the context of the decision and are to the disadvantage of the plaintiff.

BGH NJW 1998, 751, BGH, Decision of 16 October 1997 – III ZR 23/96 (Köln)

Facts

The plaintiff was until the end of 1988 a member of the board of directors of the KHG AG. On the application of the state prosecutor, the Amtsgericht (district court) ordered the arrest on the 27th February 1990 of the plaintiff and others for suspected breach of trust (Untreue) to the detriment of KHD. He was arrested on the 14th March 1990 in Italy, and brought to Germany. On the 11th May 1990 he was released from custody on conditions. The order for arrest was later revoked and the investigatory proceedings against the plaintiff discontinued. The order for arrest was based effectively on an accusation by B (who himself was in custody awaiting trial). B had claimed that he had arranged with the plaintiff at a hunting event in the Westerwald in 1983 to manipulate accounts for wood deliveries to the detriment of KHD ("the hunting hide agreement"); and that the plaintiff had received substantial sums of money for this. This accusation was substantially incorrect. At the time of his arrest the plaintiff was also managing director of the V-GmbH and had a consultancy contract with the P firm, at an annual fee of 50,180 DM. This firm terminated the contract on the 11th May 1990 with immediate effect after the press had reported the arrest of the plaintiff. On the 15th May 1990, the plaintiff and the V-GmbH agreed to cancel the managing director's contract. The Amtsgericht decided that the plaintiff should be compensated for the harm resulting from

*the arrest from the 14th March to the 11th May 1990 in accordance
with the Compensation for Measures related to Criminal Prosecution
Act. The plaintiff claimed as material harm his loss of earnings with
the V GmbH and the P firm and legal and other expenses. The
Ministry of Justice of the defendant state (Land) accepted liability for
material harm in the sum of 16,664.64 DM. This sum consisted of
part of the legal and other expenses.*

*In the present claim the plaintiff seeks amongst other things com-
pensation for loss of earnings due to the termination of the consultancy contract with the P firm, further legal costs and a finding that
any further harm resulting from the termination of the consultancy
contract should be compensated.*

Grounds

II. The investigating state prosecutor when examining whether
an order for arrest should be made against the plaintiff, stated
there was strong suspicion of breach of trust (§ 266 of the
Criminal Code and § 112(1) sentence 1 of the Criminal
Procedure Code). The appeal court regarded this as a culpable
violation of official duty on his part. That satisfies legal examination in the end result.

1. According to the case law of the Senate certain measures by
the state prosecutor, which include application for issue of an
order for an arrest are not to be examined in official liability proceedings for their "correctness" but only as to whether they are
justifiable [references omitted].

Proceeding from this legal principle, the appeal court held that
the assumption by the state prosecutor that there was strong suspicion at that time of breach of trust by the plaintiff was unjustifiable. It interpreted the statements of B, on which the state
prosecutor principally based his assessment, as meaning that the
plaintiff and B in their conversation of August / September 1983
(the hunting hide agreement) had agreed to a future manipula-
tion of accounts. This would mean that the manipulations would
only have begun after this point in time. In reality, so the appeal
court found, it was already obvious at the point in time of the
application for the order for the arrest (on the basis of witness

140

statements and other documents on the investigatory proceedings) that accounting manipulations of this kind had been going on since the nineteen sixties. In these circumstances, the accusation made by B was incredible from the start, and the application for the order for arrest was unjustifiable.

This assessment can only be examined by the court hearing the appeal in law by considering whether the judge of fact misunderstood the concept of justifiability, violated rules of logic or general principles of experience and considered all the circumstances which were of significance for the judgment [references omitted]. The appeal in law does not reveal mistakes of this kind. Insofar as it complains of a violation of rules of logic it puts its own assessment of the facts in place of those of the appeal court in a manner which the rules about appeals in law do not permit. The procedural objections raised by the appeal in law in this connection have been examined by the Senate and not considered to be decisive. No ground was therefore found here either (§ 565 a of the Civil Procedure Code). It accordingly has been established in a binding manner that the assumption of strong suspicion on which the application by the state prosecutor for an order for arrest was based was unjustifiable and making the application for an order for arrest was therefore contrary to official duty.

2. The appeal court also, without any legal error, found the investigating state prosecutor to be culpable. In this connection it basically assumes that no blame as a rule attaches to an official if a collegial court with several legal experts sitting on it has regarded the official action as objectively lawful [references omitted]. According to the view of the appeal court, this general principle, from which the Senate has repeatedly permitted exceptions [references omitted], did not apply here. There are no legal grounds for objecting to this in the end result.

(a) The appeal court denied that the principle applied here, even though the civil chamber of the *Landgericht* regarded the conduct of the state prosecutor as justifiable and therefore as objectively in accordance with his official duties. It considered that the chamber basically proceeded in this assessment from a legally flawed approach. Whether this is correct does not need to be considered, because in any case there is another ground for the said principle not applying here.

The principle is based on the consideration that a better understanding of the law cannot as a rule be expected and demanded from an official than from a collegial court with several legal experts sitting on it [reference omitted]. This justifies a denial of culpability only in those cases in which the collegial court – after careful examination – has affirmed the legality of the official action. If on the other hand the collegial court has merely approved the action on the basis of a yardstick for testing – here the yardstick of justifiability – which is *reduced* in comparison with the official's own duty of testing, this does not necessarily mean that the conduct of the official should be assessed as lawful. Whilst therefore in cases like the present one the official himself has a duty to regulate his conduct entirely by the yardstick of legality, the judicial examination in the official liability proceedings decides merely on the basis of the reduced yardstick of justifiability whether he has acted in accordance with his official duty. In such cases the principle becomes subject to a further exception over and above the group of cases decided by the Senate so far. The defendant state cannot therefore successfully rely in the present case on the first instance judgment for saying that no accusation of culpability can be levelled at the investigating state prosecutor.

(b) The appeal court was also right in not considering itself to be required to apply the general principle by the decision of the 14th great criminal chamber of the *Landgericht* in the proceedings concerning the complaint about arrest. This is because a comprehensive and careful examination of the issue of lawfulness which could justify the application of the principle did not, according to the findings of the appeal court, take place in those proceedings. The appeal court explained in this respect, in its assessment as a judge of fact of the circumstances which influenced the proceedings concerning the complaint about arrest, that the criminal chamber had "tested in an extremely summary fashion" the question of strong suspicion "and instead of this, concentrated on the question of the . . . danger of flight". It concludes this from the fact that the decision by the chamber was issued on the same day as the decision by the *Amtsgericht* that there would be no review. In a "fast-track" procedure of this kind, a dependable formation of opinion by the collegial court was not possible in the light of the scope of the documentation. This assessment, the real core of which was not addressed by the appeal in law, is confirmed by the content of the decision about the complaint:

The *Amtsgericht* in the original order for arrest had suspended its execution. The state prosecution service complaint against this only disputed the exemption from arrest. The attention of the criminal chamber was therefore principally directed to the question of whether the danger of flight was to be assessed as so small that a suspension of execution should be considered. It is true that the criminal chamber was also obliged of its own motion to examine the question of strong suspicion. In this respect however it contented itself, according to the wording of its decision, with referring to the order for arrest and pointing out that this was essentially based on the testimony of the co-accused B, who severely incriminated the plaintiff. This reasoning makes it clear that the assessment of strong suspicion which influenced the order for arrest and formed the basis of the application for the order for arrest, and which the appeal court regarded without any legal error as unjustifiable, has left its mark on the decision by the *Landgericht* about the complaint.

On the basis of the findings made by the appeal court the starting point must accordingly be that the criminal chamber did not assess the established facts of the case carefully and exhaustively; or it formed its conclusion that there was strong suspicion from facts established on the basis of procedural irregularity. In such cases the general principle does not apply [references omitted].

3. The statements of the appeal court about the extent of the claim for official liability awarded to the plaintiff and about the calculation of the period covered by the declaration are not challenged by the appeal in law.

OLG Oldenburg VersR 1991, 306, (175) OLG Oldenburg, Judgment of 20 May 1988 (6 U 28/88)

Facts

On the 22nd December 1982, the plaintiff was committed to the secure section of the state (Land) hospital X at the request of the defendant. On the same day the defendant applied for committal of the plaintiff in accordance with §§ 10 ff. of the PsychKG ND. The medical opinion supporting the application diagnosed "paranoia (delusions of jealousy and persecution)". It said the illness was a risk to the plaintiff and others. Dr D, the defendant's medical officer, signed the opinion after telephone conversations with the doctor in attendance, Dr F, who also signed it. Dr D did not personally examine the plaintiff.

The Amtsgericht (district court) decided on the 23rd December 1982 to commit the plaintiff for a maximum of six weeks for observation. From the 29th December 1982 to the 4th January 1983 the hospital gave him leave of absence. He lodged a complaint, and the Landgericht quashed the committal decision on the 13th January 1983.

By a letter of the 18th July 1983 the defendant's road traffic division asked the plaintiff to submit a medico-psychological report about his fitness to drive. He did not reply, so the defendant withdrew his driving licence on the 29th August 1983. It did not order immediate implementation of this decision. The Oberverwaltungsgericht (upper administrative court) quashed the defendant's decision, because the plaintiff had not been proved unfit to drive. No severe mental illness had been shown for the period from the end of 1982 to the beginning of 1983. The plaintiff was justified in refusing to undergo the examination demanded.

The plaintiff now claimed from the defendant payment of compensation for distress estimated at 100,000 DM, and payment of loss of earnings of 140,626.60 DM. He also wanted a declaration that the defendant was obliged to compensate for future material harm.

The plaintiff claimed that the medical officer, who had approved the committal without making his own investigation, and the official in the administrative office, who had ordered the committal without a previous court decision, had violated their official duties. There was no risk to either to the plaintiff himself or others. This was not the typical consequence of a paranoia, and the official would have realised this if he had shown proper care. Even the withdrawal of the driving licence had been a breach of duty because it had been based on the unlawful provisional committal (or the temporary committal) without a proper investigation. The withdrawal of the driving licence had resulted in the plaintiff losing his job.

(The Bundesgerichtshof in its decision of the 29th March 1990 (III ZR 160/88) (BGH VersR 1991, 308) rejected the plaintiff's appeal in law against the judgment set out here).

Reasons

The plaintiff has a claim against the defendant for compensation for distress in the sum of 5000 DM for unlawful deprivation of freedom. On the other hand he cannot ask for compensation for his loss of earnings because it cannot be established that the loss claimed was caused by a culpable violation by the defendant of official duty. The plaintiff's claim for a declaration in relation to his future harm is accordingly likewise unfounded.

1. The prerequisites for the granting of compensation for distress in accordance with § 847 of the BGB are present. The plaintiff has been deprived of freedom by a tort by the defendant in the sense of § 839 of the BGB in combination with Art 34 of the Basic Law. The medical officer in the service of the defendant, Dr D has violated an official duty owed by him to the plaintiff in that he signed a medical certificate for the instigation of the committal procedure, without making it sufficiently clear that the findings of Dr F which formed the basis of it had been made several days before the submission of the opinion. Therefore a provisional committal of the plaintiff on this basis in accordance with § 16 of the PsychKG ND could not be considered. The opinion which was sent to the administrative section of the defendant on the 22nd December 1982 contains no date. Nor can it be deduced from the text of the opinion when

the plaintiff was examined and when the findings which were decisive for the opinion were ascertained.

And yet the opinion form signed by the medical officer gives the impression that it was filled up immediately after the ascertaining of the findings. This is because in the first line (which contains the word "Urgent" in bold) and in the text of the request before the signatures of the doctors (which asks for an immediate decision) it is made clear that the committal procedure could not be postponed and that the medical experts had also taken that into acount.

But actually the plaintiff had last spoken with the doctor in attendance, Dr F, on the 15th December 1982, as the medical officer indicated in his testimony in the investigatory proceedings. Further contacts after this point in time, for instance on the 21st December 1982, indisputably broke down. The medical officer himself did not examine the plaintiff at any time.

The medical officer was under a duty to provide appropriate explanations in his area of work and therefore in particular in the content of the opinion. It was true that it was not part of the responsibility of the medical officer to arrange directly for the committal of the person affected or to apply to the court. It should however have been obvious to him that the competent official in the administrative section of the defendant would rely on the statement by the doctors and because of the urgency of the matter would very probably first of all arrange for a provisional committal in accordance with § 16 of the PsychKG ND. It was therefore a duty of the medical officer, which he owed to the person affected, to ensure that this foreseeable unlawful provisional committal did not take place.

The violation of duty by the medical officer led with adequate causality to the unlawful deprivation of the plaintiff's freedom. The responsible officer in the administrative office relied on the statements in the opinion without himself investigating at what point in time the findings were ascertained and he arranged for a provisional committal of the plaintiff in accordance with § 16 of the PsychKG ND.

It is true that the defendant has not expressly issued a formal administrative act in respect of the committal. The plaintiff was however indisputedly moved to the state hospital X with the official assistance of the police before the issuing of the judicial committal decision. This amounts to conclusive conduct (*schlüssiges Handeln*) on the part of the defendant which was made known to the plaintiff when it was carried out. If the point in time when the findings were ascertained had been known to the official of the administrative office, the provisional committal would not have taken place, since it must be assumed that the authorities would act in accordance with their duties.

It can be left open whether the plaintiff, had the medical officer acted lawfully, would possibly on the 22nd December 1982 have been examined again, perhaps compulsorily, whether the diagnosis would have been confirmed and whether he then would likewise have been provisionally committed. This is because the defendant cannot rely on the fact that it could have achieved the deprivation of freedom in a lawful manner which would have not formed the basis of a duty to compensate (reliance on lawful alternative action).

When a person causes harm by a breach of duty, the question of the extent to which the consequences of his conduct can rightly be assessed as attributable to him is to be answered according to the protective purpose of the violated norm involved [references omitted]. In the present case, there has been a violation of the conditions laid down in § 16 of the PsychKG ND. This provision is the expression of a constitutional guarantee according to which the state is only permitted to limit the freedom of a person on the basis of a formal statute and only if it takes into account the provisos described in it (Arts 2 and 104 of the Basic Law).

The protective purpose of the statute thus lies in permitting a deprivation of freedom only under the conditions prescribed in it. In this particular case it should also be ensured that, up to a point directly before the decision to commit, the state of health of the person concerned has not improved to such an extent that deprivation of freedom is no longer justified. The special urgency of immediate deprivation of freedom must thus be accepted in each case. Unless it is certain that the state of health will continue, the deprivation of freedom must not occur.

It is therefore a question of a fundamental protective norm to guarantee the rights of the citizen, which is not allowed to lose its significance in the context of compensation law just because some form of alternative action would have been lawful [references omitted].

On the same basis the argument of the *Landgericht* that the *Amtsgericht*, if it *had* been in a position to make a decision on the relevant day, would have ordered the committal cannot exonerate the defendant either. Here also the protective purpose of the violated norm excludes appeal to lawful alternative action.

The medical officer has also acted culpably. By using the required care, he could recognise and foresee that the official of the administrative section would see himself as compelled, on the basis of the dangerous situation for the plaintiff and other third parties as certified in the opinion, not only to arrange for a judicial committal but also to order immediately a provisional committal in accordance with § 16 of the PsychKG ND to avert the danger. (Details are given).

The defendant must therefore pay to the plaintiff compensation for distress for the non-material detriments suffered in consequence of the deprivation of freedom. In this connection, when calculating the amount of the damages for distress not only must the length of time of the provisional committal to be taken into account, but also that of the judicial committal. This is because it can be assumed that the court also would have come to another conclusion in its decision in accordance with § 15 of the PsychKG ND if it had known that the last examination of the plaintiff by the medical expert had taken place a week ago.

Taking into account all the circumstances, damages for distress of 5000 DM seem fair but also sufficient to the Senate. The plaintiff was committed from the 22nd to the 29th December 1982. According to his own account he was given leave of absence on the 29th December 1982 so that the consequences of the deprivation of freedom did not continue beyond this point in time. At the most the possibility remained of the further detriment of revocation of the leave of absence. This however did not happen. Long term harm to the plaintiff did not therefore occur.

Even if freedom is to be regarded as a legal interest worthy of the highest protection, the plaintiff's ideas about compensation (100,00 DM) for distress seem greatly exaggerated. They bear no relationship to the compensation which is payable for unjustified criminal arrest. Admittedly the plaintiff was temporarily arrested by the police in order to implement the committal order, and these circumstances and the fact of committal in his home town have been talked about and have had a disadvantageous effect on his social relationships and his reputation. But even bearing these matters in mind compensation for distress in the approved sum is the most that should be considered.

The claim of the plaintiff is not excluded by § 839 (1) sentence 2 of the BGB. Firstly Dr D has disregarded the protective provisions of PsychKG ND not merely negligently but (at least) grossly negligently. Besides this the plaintiff has no other option for compensation available.

The issue of whether a possibility exists of obtaining compensation from the state can remain open, as this is also a public law body and the claim would therefore likewise be directed against the public sector; and it is necessary to proceed on the basis of the unity of the public sector [reference omitted]. The plaintiff can also not claim against the other medical expert, Dr F. (Details are given).

II. On the other hand the plaintiff has no claim against the defendant under § 839 of the BGB and Art 34 of the Basic Law to compensation for his loss of earnings nor to a declaration that the defendant is obliged to compensate for future harm. This is because it can neither be established that the defendant has culpably violated an official duty in taking proceedings for withdrawal of the driving licence nor that the alleged harm to the plaintiff arose as a consequence of the measures taken by the defendant.

In the present case no blame, as the *Landgericht* has already pertinently explained, attaches to the defendant in any case, since in relation to this measure, a collegial court in which three professional judges sat, namely the *Verwaltungsgericht*, has adjudged its conduct to be objectively justified. The conditions developed in this respect for justifying a denial of the culpability of the office holder are present. The *Verwaltungsgericht* in its decision used the right facts as a basis, evaluated these carefully and in its assessment of the legal situation neither misjudged clear and unambiguous rules nor blatantly falsely interpreted unambiguous rules.

With reference to the grounds of the court decision of the 27th November 1984 the *Verwaltungsgericht* proceeding on the basis of the relevant provisions ($\S\S$ 4(1) of the Implementation of Punishment Act (*StVG*) and 15b(1) of the Road Traffic Licences Order (*StVZO*)) looked carefully at the documents which were available about the plaintiff's psychological condition and came to the conclusion that they justified doubts about the fitness of the plaintiff to drive.

It accepted that this, together with the plaintiff's lack of preparedness to dispel the doubts by producing a medico-psychological opinion, justifies the conclusion that the plaintiff wanted to conceal defects which made him unfit to drive a vehicle. One must therefore, so it explained, proceed on the basis of his unsuitability to drive vehicles. These considerations of the *Verwaltungsgericht* do not violate rules of logic. The legal views referred to are at least defensible, taking into consideration the provisions cited.

Beside this it is not evident that the withdrawal of the driving licence was the cause of the harm claimed by the plaintiff. (Details are given).

ZfJ 84 no. 11/97 p.433 – OLG Hamm, 20th November 1996 (11 U 61/96)[4]

Facts

K was born in February 1976. The plaintiff was her mother and the sole person entitled to look after her.

In November 1992 K presented herself at the Youth Welfare Department of the defendant district and told them about recent

[4] Translated by Mr Raymond Youngs, Southampton Institute.

domestic difficulties with the plaintiff. (K had already been accommodated for a time by the Youth Welfare Department in the children's home B in M, in early 1991). She explained to the officer in charge, Me, that she could not stand things at home any more. She refused a mediation interview with the plaintiff. But K and the plaintiff had a conversation of at least one and a half hours on the morning of the 17th November 1992. Me was present for part of the time. No settlement was reached.

The Youth Welfare Department applied to the Guardianship Court C, which arranged a hearing on the afternoon of the 17th November 1992. K was heard first, and she repeated to the judge her statements contained in the report of the Youth Welfare Department, and said she did not want to go back home. Then the plaintiff was heard. The Guardianship Court tried to arrange a settlement between K and the plaintiff, but failed. It made a temporary order taking away the plaintiff's right to determine K's place of residence, and transferring this to the Youth Welfare Department as guardian.

K was then accommodated by the Youth Welfare Department at first in the Youth Protection Centre in D and from the 10th December 1992 in the children's home B in M. On the 5th September 1993 K left the home of her own accord and returned to the plaintiff.

On the 27th September 1993 the Guardianship Court transferred full custody rights back to the plaintiff. But because of a new argument, the plaintiff finally excluded K from home on the 11th November 1993. The two have since lived separately from one another.

The plaintiff lodged a complaint against the decision of the Guardianship Court. This was rejected by the Landgericht M on the 2nd July 1993 because K's wish not to return home had to be respected.

The plaintiff claimed compensation from the defendant district including damages for distress because the Youth Welfare Department deprived her of K in a manner contrary to their official duty.

The action and the appeal were unsuccessful.

Reasons

The prerequisites for a claim for official liability under §§ 839 and 847 of the BGB in combination with Art 34 of the GG, which is the only for basis a claim to be considered here, are not present.

I. The work and tasks of youth assistance – and along with this the official duties of the Youth Welfare Department – arise from § 2 of the KJHG. This work includes amongst other things educational assistance and supplementary services (§§ 2 (2) nos. 4, 27–37, 39 and 40 KJHG), and the other tasks include amongst other things taking children and young people into care (§§ 2 (3) Nos. 1 and 42 KJHG SGB VIII).

On this basis, the Youth Welfare Department of the defendant district has not violated any official duties which could be the cause of the plaintiff's alleged harm.

1. The decision of the Youth Welfare Department to take K into care on the 16th November 1992 and to seek a decision of the Guardianship Court on the 17th November 1992 was in accordance with their official duty.

a) According to § 42 (2) of the KJHG the Youth Welfare Department is under a duty to take a young person into care if he or she asks for this. It has to inform the person having custody about the taking into care without delay.

These prerequisites are fulfilled in the present case. K asked to be taken into care by the Youth Welfare Department of the defendant district on the 16th November as a so-called "voluntary admission". The duty of the Youth Welfare Department to take into care applies without any limitation, regardless of the grounds on which the young person asks for care and of whether these grounds are convincing; the requirements to be placed on the content of these grounds must not be too high [references omitted].

The plaintiff as the person having custody had unquestionably been notified of the taking into care, and in this connection it does not matter for the purpose of the decision whether this notification was based on her own initiative or on that of the Youth Welfare Department.

b) According to § 42 (2) sentence 3 of the KJHG the Youth Welfare Department must, if the person having custody challenges the taking into care, either hand the young person over to the person having custody (option 1) or obtain a decision by the Guardianship Court about the necessary measures for the welfare of the young person (option 2). These steps must take place without delay.

aa) Unquestionably, the plaintiff challenged the taking into care in the conversation on the morning of the 17th November 1992. She accuses the Youth Welfare Department of not having kept the appointment arranged at 12 o'clock for the continuation of the discussion, but it is not evident that this would have made a difference in the context of the plaintiff's challenge. On the evidence of the memorandum of the hearing before the Guardianship Court, the plaintiff still stated to the court that she did not agree with the taking into care - at any rate not unconditionally.

bb) In this situation, the Youth Welfare Department was under a duty to make an "immediate" decision. No objection can be raised to the fact that it chose, out of the two alternatives to be considered, not to hand K over to the plaintiff, but to invoke the Guardianship Court. This was in accordance with their official duty.

In the literature [reference omitted] the view is taken that when a person having custody challenges a taking into care, the Youth Welfare Department is always obliged to bring in the Guardianship Court even if the Department considers there is no danger to the child's welfare. According to another view [reference omitted] the Youth Welfare Department only needs to obtain a decision of the Guardianship Court (and also must, without there being any discretion) if the welfare of the young person is endangered. Both opinions lead here to the same conclusion.

In making its decision, the Youth Welfare Department could (and had to) take into account that help for K's upbringing had already been necessary (in January/February 1991), that there were unquestionably school, alcohol and drug problems and that again K absolutely refused to go back home. As K was at that time already nearly 17 years old, the Youth Welfare Department could take this refusal seriously.

Assuming a danger to the child's welfare in this situation, and bringing in the Guardianship Court, were not contrary to the Youth Welfare Department's official duty. It could regard the decisions of the Guardianship Court and of the Landgericht based on §§ 1666 and 1666a of the BGB (endangering of child's welfare) as retrospectively confirming this assumption. The urgency of the measures to be taken by the Youth Welfare Department also did not permit – contrary to the view of the plaintiff – the making of further enquiries, in particular the hearing of the witnesses who were later heard by the Guardianship Court. The necessary elucidation of the matter was ensured because the Guardianship Court was under a duty to investigate of its own motion (§ 12 of the FGG).

2. The Youth Welfare Department would certainly have acted contrary to its official duty if it had "wangled" the right to determine K's accommodation by – as the plaintiff claims – influencing K by insinuation to make untrue statements to the Guardianship Court.

But the plaintiff has not substantiated this sweeping accusation in any greater detail, either in writing or at her examination in accordance with § 141 of the Civil Procedure Code at the Senate's hearing; so taking evidence did need to be considered here. The plaintiff has merely asserted that the Youth Welfare Department stated to K that she must only stick to her point of view and say that she did not want to return home in any circumstances. The Senate cannot see any improper influencing of K in this.

The decision of the Guardianship Court is based in substance on K's wish, as stated to it, that she did not want to go back home. This stated wish was not however inconsistent with the truth.

The plaintiff herself admitted on her personal examination

before the Senate that K, at the point in time in question, did not in fact want to go back home and that even in the conversation on the morning of the 17th November 1992 there were no prospects of this. Moreover, K stated this wish approximately eight months later to the Complaints Chamber of the Landgericht. There is no allegation that the facts of the case were presented to the Guardianship Court in some other way which was inconsistent with the truth and based on improper influence by the Youth Welfare Department.

3. The Youth Welfare Department has also not violated its official duties by accommodating K after the decision of the Guardianship Court, at first in the Youth Protection Centre Ka in D and afterwards in the children's home B in M.

a) On the basis of the decision of the Guardianship Court, the right to determine K's place of residence was provisionally transferred to the Youth Welfare Department as guardian (§§ 1631(1), 1666 and 1666a of the BGB). The Youth Welfare Department could therefore decide on K's place of residence without the agreement of the plaintiff [reference omitted]. The right to determine a place of residence also includes the authority to exercise care of the person concerned to the extent necessary for a parent. This includes entrusting the person to a family or – as here – the houseparents in a home. This authority is part of the right to determine the place of residence.

b) Besides this, the plaintiff shows no alternative to accommodation in a home – which was in any case only provisional for the period of the temporary order – especially as she and K could not agree at the hearing before the Guardianship Court on accommodation with another appropriate care person. Accommodation with the plaintiff herself was out of the question as a serious alternative after the Guardianship Court had just taken this aspect of guardianship away from her.

4. Finally it cannot be established that the Youth Welfare Department violated its official duty just because it did not, following the decision of the Guardianship Court, provide any services – additionally to accommodation in the home – under § 2(2) of the KJHG.

a) In this connection, the Senate can leave open the question of whether the Youth Welfare Department, under the given circumstances of the plaintiff, ought to have offered such services, namely educational assistance (§ 27 of the KJHG) educational advice (§ 28 of the KJHG) or socio-pedagogical family assistance (§ 31 of the KJHG). The Senate can therefore also leave open the question of whether it was due to lack of readiness on the part of the Youth Welfare Department or on the part of the plaintiff that this did not occur; even at the Senate hearing this could not be resolved by examination of the parties on both sides.

b) But this does not need to be resolved in order to decide the legal dispute; that is why it is not necessary to go into the question of whether the memoranda submitted by the defendant district were – as the plaintiff asserts – made out after the event or not. Because even if the Youth Welfare Department breached its duty in not offering to the plaintiff and K services in accordance with § 2(2) of the KJHG, it cannot be established within the framework of the necessary examination of causality that matters would then have taken such a course that the harm which is the subject of the plaintiff's claim would not have arisen.

aa) Even according to the plaintiff's own allegation, no sufficient grounds were present for saying that if services under § 2(2) of the KJHG had been obtained the relationship between the plaintiff and K would have improved. The plaintiff herself described K as a "very egocentric girl with a very strongly demanding nature". K's behaviour, in so far as this is of importance for the resolution of the legal dispute, confirms the plaintiff's own assessment. Within the framework of § 287 of the Civil Procedure Code, which is to be applied here, success from services under § 2(2) of the KJHG cannot in any case be established or even assumed; demonstrating this is the responsibility of the plaintiff who is under a duty of explanation and proof in respect of causality.

bb) Even if a different view is taken, there is nothing to indicate within the framework of § 287 of the Civil Procedure Code that services under § 2(2) of the KJHG would have succeeded so quickly that the harm which is the subject of the plaintiff's claim would thereby have been avoided or at least reduced; demonstrating this also falls to the plaintiff who is under a duty of explanation and proof in respect of it.

The harm to her reputation which the plaintiff asserts – and the sale of her house in H associated with this – is based only on the taking into care under § 42(2) of the KJHG, the ensuing deprivation of the right to determine the place of residence by the Guardianship Court and the subsequent accommodation of K in the Youth Protection Centre Ka and in the children's home B. Even the legal costs and the costs of visits and telephone calls arose exclusively in connection with the taking into care, the deprivation of the right of determination of the place of residence and the accommodation. This harm would therefore also not have been avoided by additional services by the Youth Welfare Department under § 2(2) of the KJHG. The same applies for the impairment which the plaintiff claimed occurred to her health. Apart from the fact that, according to the statements of the plaintiff to the expert D, this impairment must for the most part have existed previously, there is nothing to indicate that it would have been avoided or even significantly reduced by services by the Youth Welfare Department under § 2(2) of the KJHG.

FamRZ 1993, 704[5]

The plaintiff married couple and their adopted son, the former third plaintiff, sought compensation from the defendant town because of violation of official duty in connection with an adoption placement.

Grounds

The appeal of the defendant is permissible, but unsuccessful.

[5] Translated by Mr Raymond Youngs, Southampton Institute.

I.

The *Landgericht* was correct in accepting the plaintiffs' claims for official liability against the defendant on the basis of § 839 of the BGB in combination with Art 34 of the GG and allowed the demands for payment and a declaration.

1. The appropriate officials who were involved in preparing and carrying out an adoption by the plaintiffs have negligently violated their official duties owed to the plaintiffs by not informing them that there was a suspicion that the child N, who was very disturbed, was mentally retarded.

a) It is necessary to proceed on the basis that the actions of the Youth Welfare Department in the area of adoption placement, even according to the legal situation in the years 1981 to 1983 (which is the relevant period here), are the exercise of public office in the sense of Art 34 of the GG [reference omitted]. Action in exercise of public office occurs if the real objective in the context of which the official is acting is part of the area of sovereign activity of a public body. There must also be an internal and external connection between this objective and the act (or omission) which causes the damage, so that the act (or omission) must also be regarded as belonging to this area of sovereign activity [reference omitted]. Such a connection exists for the actions of the Youth Welfare Department in the framework of adoption placement. According to § 2(1) sentence 1 of the Adoption Placement Act in its 2nd July 1976 version [reference omitted] adoption placement is a task for the Youth Welfare Department (and for the State (Land) Youth Welfare Department). Adoption placement is bringing together children under the age of majority and persons who want to adopt a child (adoption applicants) with the object of adopting it as well as providing the evidence of adoption (§ 1 of the Adoption Placement Act). Leaving exceptions aside, the Youth Welfare Departments who have set up an Adoption Placement Office and the State Youth Welfare Departments have a placement monopoly (§§ 2(1) sentence 2 and 5(1) of the Adoption Placement Act). The actions of the Youth Welfare Department in the area of adoption placement are accordingly a public task, the purpose of which is to find appropriate and suitable parents who are prepared to adopt for a child who does not have the care of its natural parents. These actions are therefore to assist the young.

b) The employees of the Youth Welfare Department of the defendant acted contrary to their official duty because they neglected to inform the plaintiffs as adoption applicants about the suspicion of mental retardation due to brain damage which was known to them and not dispelled. The content and scope of the official duties of a public employee are determined by the provisions regulating the area of his tasks and duties, whether they are statutes, regulations, administrative provisions or individual directions in the context of employment; and from the kind of tasks to be carried out [reference omitted]. The duty to inform the plaintiffs about the suspicion which existed arose in the present case from the kind of tasks to be carried out by the officials within the framework of the adoption placement.

The Adoption Placement Act itself admittedly contains no express regulations which make it a duty of the Adoption Placement Office to inform the adoption applicants about the state of health of the child to be adopted. However, according to § 7(1) sentence 1 of the Adoption Placement Act, the Adoption Placement Office must make without delay the enquiries which are necessary for preparing for a placement, and these must also extend to the state of health of the child. Admittedly the implementation regulations provided for in § 7(2) of the Adoption Placement Act have not so far been made. But the Working Group of the State Youth Welfare Departments has worked out guidelines which at that time applied in the version of the 3rd edition of 1966 and which provided in para 2.22 that the physical as well as the mental and psychological state of health of the child was to be ascertained by a doctor experienced in these areas – if possible a paediatrician or a psychiatrist specialising in the young. Further, it says in para 2.23(1) that an investigation by a specialist, if necessary even in-patient observation, was to be arranged if inquiries revealed that the child has educational difficulties, suspicion of illness or unexplained abnormalities. Even if these guidelines (which were replaced in the meantime by the "Recommendations of the Federal Working Group of State Youth Welfare Departments and Non-local Education Committees on Adoption Placement" – Version of the 28th November 1988) were merely for practical work assistance, and they therefore did not represent legal or administrative provisions, they nevertheless express what a proper individual adoption placement requires. This is that the adoption applicants should be able to decide to adopt a child in the knowledge of all important facts, so that a successful parent-child relationship which is free from anxiety can come into existence for the welfare of the child. § 9(1) of the Adoption Placement Act which makes it a duty of the Adoption Placement Office to give detailed advice and support not only to the child and its natural parents but also to the adopters is in harmony with this. It follows from the duty of inquiry mentioned above (§ 7(1) of the Adoption Placement Act) as well as from the duty of advice owed by the Adoption Placement Office (§ 9(1) of the Adoption Placement Act) that the adoption applicants have a right to be notified of all the relevant circumstances affecting the child, and especially of suspicion of an illness [reference omitted]. The guidelines of the Working Group of the State Youth Welfare Departments, if and so far as they required that the state of health of the child was to be established by medical examination, therefore corresponded with these requirements. Admittedly the adoption of children with physical or mental peculiarities should also be facilitated. But that can only be considered if the adopters feel they are ready for this in the knowledge of all the circumstances and the consequences of their decision (para 2.23(2) of the Guidelines).

c) The defendant's officials knew of the suspicion of mental retardation on the basis of brain damage parentally or in early childhood.

That emerges clearly from the memorandum by the witness N dated 7th October 1981, in which the possibility of mental retardation on the basis of inborn brain damage was expressly taken into consideration. Even the official doctor, Dr M, who had examined the child, regarded the mental retardation as so significant that, according to the memorandum of the witness M referred to above, she thought a "very meticulous examination" in a hospital was necessary. Arrangements were consequently made to examine the child in the children's clinic B; but this did not happen. But the doctors at the children's clinic at the St V hospital in P, according to their letter of the 11th November 1981, of which the defendant's Youth Welfare Department received a copy, diagnosed not only wildness and behavioural disturbance in the child but also the suspicion of mental retardation, which could have meant that this retardation had its cause in brain damage. The appropriate officials could not regard this suspicion of mental retardation as dispelled by the interim report of the 8th December 1981 by the witness T. The only thing which emerged from this report was that a particular positive development had occurred on the basis of psychotherapeutic treatment by the witness T. No grounds for saying that N had been subjected to a detailed specialist examination were revealed by the interim report. T made no comment at all in it on the question of mental retardation based on brain damage. From the outcome of the evidence taken by the Senate, it is not possible to proceed on the basis that the witness T (who in any case was not a neurologist or a psychiatrist, but a psychologist) explained to the witness M (as it says in her memorandum of the 4th December 1981) that the child had a normal intelligence and no mental handicap could be established. The witnesses T and M who were heard on this issue made contradictory statements. The witness T denied having expressed himself in this way to the witness M. But even if T had so expressed himself to the witness M, as she describes, the employees of the defendant cannot reassure themselves by saying that the suspicion of mental retardation was dispelled. This is because the statement by T did not in any case mean anything more than that he – as a psychologist – had not established any such damage.

would not have dispelled the suspicion. But even in the latter case, the plaintiffs would have refrained from adopting the child N because of the risk of adopting a mentally handicapped child. As they did not want to adopt such a child, they would also not have taken the risk of possibly having to bear the responsibility and burdens of such a child.

5. a) The plaintiff can claim from the defendant compensation for her loss of earnings in the undisputed sum of 30,610.44 DM. The plaintiffs have, without being contradicted, argued that the plaintiff giving up her job had been a prerequisite for the adoption placement. According to the testimony of the plaintiff, which likewise remained uncontradicted, when she gave evidence at the Senate hearing of the 15th July 1992, she had given up her job on the 16th December 1981, when the plaintiffs took N into their care. The plaintiff would not have suffered loss of earnings if the defendant's officials had fulfilled the duty to inform which they owed to the plaintiffs; because then no adoption would have taken place and the plaintiff would not have needed to give up her job for the time being. The defendant, in this respect under a duty of explanation, has not substantiated that the plaintiffs, who certainly wanted to adopt a child, would have had the actual opportunity before the lapse of 19 months – reckoned from the 16th December 1981 – to adopt another child, and that the loss of earnings would therefore still have arisen in whole or in part.

b) On the same grounds the court costs and notarial expenses borne by the plaintiff in the undisputed sum of 91.59 DM are to be compensated.

6. The claim for a declaration by the plaintiffs in relation to the duty of the defendant to compensate for possible future harm is also well founded. The prerequisite for the issue of a declaratory judgment is merely that there is a certain probability that claims have arisen or could arise from the legal relationship which is to be established [reference omitted]. The prerequisite is fulfilled in this case. The future harm exists predominantly in the expenditure on maintenance which the plaintiffs must provide for the handicapped child, possibly for the whole of its life. The duty to

compensate for harm is not limited to the additional expenditure on maintenance which arises through the special needs of a mentally handicapped child. The defendant must instead reimburse the plaintiffs for the whole of the expenditure on maintenance. The provision of information about all the important facts and circumstances of the adoption to the adoption applicants which was due from the employees of the Youth Employment Department is not only to protect them from the additional expenditure which they incur for the maintenance of a handicapped or sick child. The fulfilment of the duty to give information is also to ensure freedom of decision by the adoption applicants, and this consists of not adopting a mentally handicapped child at all. If such a child is adopted, the risk of providing full maintenance has been realised, and fulfilment of the duty to provide information should protect the adopters from this. In this respect the legal situation is similar to the one which arises when a doctor advises a pregnant woman during early pregnancy incorrectly or incompletely about the possibilities on early recognition of damage to the foetus which would have provided legal justification for the wish of the mother to terminate the pregnancy. Even in this case, the BGH has not limited the claim of the parents to compensation for harm to the additional expenditure on maintenance, but extended it to the complete maintenance requirement for the child who has been harmed [reference omitted]. In this case, the issue cannot be decided otherwise.

II.

No contributory fault for the origination of the harm can be laid at the door of the plaintiffs in connection with the adoption of the child N (§ 254(1) of the BGB).

III.

The appeal is accordingly rejected.

(Submitted by Judge Müller, OLG Hamm)

Bundesgerictshof (Third Civil Division) 27 May 1963, BGHZ 39, 358 = NJW 1963, 1821 = JZ 63, 707 (with a critical note by H H Rupp = VersR 1963, 973)[6]

The plaintiff site-owner claimed damages from a local authority, which had issued a building permit without adequately checking the architect's calculations regarding the load-bearing capacity of the foundations, as marked on the plan. Because of this error, the building collapsed while in process of construction, and both the builder and the architect were insolvent. The trial court dismissed the plaintiff's claim and his appeal was also dismissed for the following reasons.

Reasons

1. The trial court was correct to hold that in checking and authorising the plans for the building, the supervisory authorities are exercising a governmental function. In consequence, as the Appeal Court agrees, the plaintiff's claim against the defendant can be based only on the rules relating to the liability of officials (BGB, § 839 in connection with GG, Article 34); it must be shown that one of the defendant local authority officials in the exercise of the public function attributed to him was in breach of an official duty which he owed to the plaintiff . . .

2. In approaching the question whether, in giving building permission when it should not have done so, the local authority was in breach of official duties owed to the plaintiff, the trial court correctly started by considering the purpose served by the official duty [reference]. In the first instance, official duties are imposed in the interest of the state and the public. If the sole function of an official duty is to promote public order, the general interest of the commonwealth in orderly and proper government, the satisfaction of exigencies within the service, or the maintenance of a properly organised and functioning adminis-

[6] Translated by Mr Tony Weir, Trinity College, Cambridge and reprinted from Basil Markesinis, *The German Law of Obligations* (3rd ed. OUP, 1997), Vol. II, *The Law of Torts* 581.

tration, then there is no question of any liability to third parties for its breach, even if its exercise has adversely affected them or their interest. Liability exists only where the official duty, which was broken, was owed by the official to the third parties themselves. Whether this is so and how wide the range of protected persons may be are questions which must be determined in accordance with the purpose served by the official duty. This purpose is to be inferred from the provisions on which the official duty is based and by which it is delimited, as well as from the particular nature of the official function in question. If, in addition to satisfying the general interest and public purposes, the official duty has the further purpose of safeguarding the interests of individuals, this is sufficient, even if the affected party had no legal claim that the official act in question be undertaken (BGHZ 35, 44, 46–47; BGH VersR 1961, 944).

Before a building permit is issued, the plans must be checked for conformity with all building regulations of public law (Provincial Building Ordinance, § 2 11). Such an investigation must encompass the structural safety of the building (Provincial Building Ordinance, §§ 15 1e, § 61); as the Court of Appeal was right to emphasise, with reference to Pfundtner/Neubert [reference omitted], concern for safety is one of its most important aims, since unsafe buildings pose a direct threat to life and health, the value of physical property and safe conduct of business. The supervision of buildings thus permits the avoidance of dangers (BGHZ 8, 97, 104; see Baltz and Fischer, *Preussiches Baupolizeirecht* 1 *ff.*). The provisions requiring the verification of the calculations concerning the load-bearing capacity of buildings are directed to the dangers, which threaten the public from the collapse of unsafe constructions. While these provisions and the official duties which they impose serve the protection of the public – the "public interest" (Baltz and Fischer, ibid.) – they also protect every individual member of the public who might be threatened by its unsafe condition, that is, every person who comes into contact with the building as inhabitant, user, visitor (RG Recht 1929, No. 757, SeuffArch 83, No. 134, JW 1936, 803, BGHZ 8, 97, I 04), neighbour (BGH VersR 1956, 447), passer-by (LM to BGB, § 839 Fe no. i), or workman, and who relies on its being safe. The owner or developer may also be a beneficiary of this protective function if he suffers damage to his body, health or property as a result of a collapse while he is visiting the building or inhabiting it, but only if the harm is a consequence of the danger from which it is the function of the official verification of the technical specifications to protect the public and hence the individual endangered. That is not the case here. It is true that the plaintiff has suffered damage as a result of the collapse of the building, but he is not a victim of the danger from which, as a member of the public, he was entitled to be protected by the official duties and the provisions which created them, since it was only the building itself and no other property of his which was damaged.

Bundesgerichtshof (Seventh Civil Division) 30 May 1963, BGHZ39.366 = NJW 1963, 1827 = VersR i963,933,1024[7]

In 1951 the plaintiff contracted with the defendant builder to have a house built on his land and, with the defendant architect, to have the construction supervised. Cracks appeared in the ceilings because the concrete used was well below the requisite strength. The plaintiff claimed damages for the reconstruction of the ceilings, which were in danger of collapse. Because he was out of time for a contract claim the plaintiff based his claim on the delictual provisions of BGB, § 823 1 and § 823 11 in connection with § 330 of the Criminal Code (STGB) or STGB, § 367, No. 15.

Reasons

The Court of Appeal was right to find that the facts disclosed no tort on which the plaintiff's claim for damages could be based.

[7] Translated by Mr Tony Weir, Trinity College, Cambridge and reprinted from Basil Markesinis, *The German Law of Obligations* (3rd ed. OUP, 1997), Vol. II, *The Law of Torts* 583.

1. There is no question of a claim for damages under BGB, § 823 I on the basis that the plaintiff's property *(Eigentum)* has been damaged by fault. The land owned by the plaintiff, as compared with what it was, has suffered no harm through the defective method of construction. Insofar as the land has been built on, as the Court of Appeal rightly stated, the plaintiff never owned it in a non-defective condition. As the building proceeded, the plaintiff's ownership attached to each part of the building as it was constructed in the condition in which it was constructed, with all the qualities and defects resulting from the incorporation of the building materials. To make someone the owner of a defective building is not to invade an already existing ownership (compare RG JW 1905, 367; OLG Karlsruhe NJW 1956, 913). The decision of the Senate in LM No. 4 to BGB, § 830 was a different case; there, defective concrete balconies which had been built onto the top storey caused the collapse of the whole building.

2. The Court of Appeal was also right to reject the claim for damages based on BGB, § 823 II in connection with STGB, § 330. Under this last-named provision a person "who in supervising or erecting a building in breach of generally recognised rules of building practice acts in such a way as to cause danger to others" is guilty of an offence. The trial court found that a danger existed within the meaning of this provision and this finding is not subject to review. But, as the Court of Appeal stated, STGB, § 330 is solely designed to protect the lives and health of individuals [references]. It is only to this extent that the provision is a protective statute whose breach can give rise to a claim for damages under BGB, § 823 II. Damages can be claimed under this text only if the harm takes the form of the invasion of a legal interest for whose protection the rule of law was enacted (BGHZ 19–114, 126; 28, 359, 365 f.). The claim before us is for compensation for harm to an interest other than the legal interest protected by STGB, § 330.

Nor is the claim for those damages justified by the consideration that the replacement of ceilings, which are in danger of collapse, is necessary to save the users of the rooms from immi-

nent danger. It still remains the case that the cost of rendering
the ceilings represents a harm, which affects only the pecuniary
interests of the plaintiff. This is evident if one imagines that a
ceiling collapses and injures an individual; then, certainly, the
harm attributable to the personal injuries must be compensated
under BGB, § 823 II and STGB, § 330; but there would still
remain the material harm requiring the replacement of the ceilings, and this would still affect only the economic interests of the
plaintiff.

3. The plaintiff finally relies on BGB, § 823 (II) in connection
with STGB, § 367 (I), No. 15. This provision provides, inter
alia, that it is an offence for a builder or building worker to con-
struct a building in deliberate deviation from the building plan
approved by the authority. According to the plaintiff, an offence
was committed because the approval of the plan is based on specific calculations, incorporated in the submission, relating to the
load-bearing capacity of the construction, and these calculations
were in turn based on the quality of the concrete to be used.

It is not necessary to decide whether the use of concrete infe-
rior to that on which the stress calculations were based consti-
tutes a deliberate deviation from the authorised plan. We agree
with the Court of Appeal that STGB, § 367 (I), No. 15 is not
designed to offer protection against harm of the sort for which
the plaintiff claims damages. It is true that in its decision
reported in BGB, LM, No. I § 823 (Bb) the Bundesgerichtshof
recognised that STGB, § 367 (I), No. 15 was a protective
statute; that case, however, involved personal injuries suffered
by a worker employed on the building site.

In the view of the Court of Appeal, STGB, § 367 I, No. 15
is like STGB, § 330 in offering protection only to the human
person. This view is open to criticism. The final Courts of
Appeal have accepted that the cognate provision of STGB,
§ 367 (I), No. 14 exists for the protection of property as well,
and that a breach of the provision may also give rise to claims
for damages in respect of property damage under BGB, § 823 II
(RGZ 51, 177–8, BGH, BGB, LM, No. 2 § 823 Bd). Both these
decisions. were concerned with harm caused to neighbouring

buildings adjoining the building site and vested in third parties.

Thus, it may be taken that the protective purpose of STGB, § 367 (1), No. 15 is also to be construed to guard against damage to property as well as damage to persons. In the present case, however, as has already been stated, there is no damage to property but a pecuniary loss attributable to the defective execution of the building work in breach of contract.